For Laur[a]

enjoy!

Best wishes

Mal.

BURNOUT

POEMS/EXPLANATIONS

Mal **Bibby**

ILLUSTRATED BY **DAVID WAYWELL**

scriblerus books

To Joyce, Sarah and James.
Love, peace, good health, and happiness to you all

www.malbibby.co.uk
www.davidwaywell.com

First published 2023
ISBN: 978-1-7384500-0-8
Typeset and designed
by Scriblerus Books
scriblerusbooks@gmail.com

scriblerus books

Contents

INTRODUCTION

I first saw Mal perform at the Shakespeare North Playhouse's 'Itch' open-mic night. He arrived late and performed last and yet, in my eyes, he still managed to win the night. I was immediately in awe of him and his performance, which was like watching a knot of funny but highly politicised anger unravel before your eyes. He made the room laugh and occasionally cheer with the kind of the poems that are rare these days, conveying a mixture of passion, humour, acute observation, as well as that quirky yet lyrical charm that's typical of so many poets from Liverpool. There's neither affectation nor pose about Mal's verse which is intensely meant and an honest representation of his character.

Getting to know Mal was one of the better things to have happened to me in 2023 and it was not long before I suggested he should produce a new book which I was more than happy to edit and illustrate. The work came at an important time for me and it was a chance to escape from a period of long grief. It also rekindled my enjoyment of illustration, even if my original plan to provide a few 'simple' doodles was quickly overrun by my enthusiasm to draw pictures with a lot more detail. But I hope the result is worth it.

Mal's poems deserve a place to shine, as does the man himself. Get to know Mal and you find a man who cares about the world and people around him. He hides neither his passion nor his politics. I think it even excuses his supporting the wrong team from Liverpool.

DW
Liverpool, 2023

JUST LIKE MONTY DON

Now the dog's dead and the mother-in-laws finally gone,
We want a garden, just like Monty Don.
When it comes to garden designs, Monty's the man,
When he sits down with his pen, he makes a really good plan.
So, upon reflection, ours wasn't such a clever idea
To flag over the grass, and sit round supping beer,
With the exception of weeds, vegetation has all but gone.
All we want is a garden, just like Monty Don.
We'd like to grow our own veg, if we could find the right place,
But there's so much accumulated shite, there's just no space.
Admittedly there are things that could be moved or maybe go
Where, when, and how, I don't even know,
Like our 'deluxe riviera style double swinging chair',
Where the Argos catalogue claimed would 'last us for years'.
Without being too specific, it's never been quite the same,
Since Uncle Alf sat on it, and terminally buckled the frame.
The patio set we got at the market, from the Indian fella,
The pole's never worked properly, and neither has the umbrella.
The shed's falling down, completely damp and rotten,
What the hell's in there? We've completely forgotten.
At thirteen, Julie's too old for that early learning three-step slide,
When she's wearing a skirt I have to cover both of my eyes.
Those three feet nettles need to be removed from below the swing,
She'll have to rub cream on her own arse if she gets another sting!
There's Nannas old mattress and the headboard off her single bed,
Propping up our Billy's 'pigeon loft', wedged behind the shed.
I've yet to see a pigeon so I've no idea what him and his girl get up to in there,
Unless she's hiding feathers and a beak underneath her long blonde hair.
How many times do we have to ask our kid to shift that wreck of a car?
That's where the Mrs wants her hot tub but I'm having my pop-up bar.
Monty always says, in his knitted jumper and baggy pants,
Make sure you find the optimum place to grow happy healthy plants.
We always blamed Nanna for that bad smell, where she used to sit,
Recent revelations proved it was next door's cat's chosen place to shit.

Poems / Explanations

Mal Bibby

Although you can't hear us Nanna, we're so sorry now we know it wasn't you
It was that cat from next door you fed, who repayed with endless piss & poo.
My mum would have loved the luxury of a garden because we lived in a flat,
So, we've bought a beautiful scented rose bush to commemorate that.
It's got the fragrance of an angel and blooms throughout the year,
We thought it would be such a lovely tribute to my mother so dear,
However, the only place available was adjacent to the old brick BBQ.
The smoke reminds me of her cremation and the roses are out of view,
Well, we're not south facing and our 'shared fence' is badly in disrepair.
I'm fed up with his claims next door of being skint. He just doesn't care,
Monty makes planning look simple, but he hasn't got neighbours like these
It's a struggle in our 10 by 5 to find a patch big enough to plant sweet peas.
Apparently, they like to climb so I've wrapped a bit of string
                                    round the washing pole
I've had to move Billy's 'mini eco system', frogsporn in
                                    the pink washing up bowl
Monty never shows where he puts his pizza oven or his bins
                                    despite 10 acres or more
We've already got green brown and grey, and any day soon
                                    it's moving up to four
To hide the bins, I've put a palm tree in the sandpit so we can
                                    pretend we're in Dubai
We've had to go plastic mind 'cos the price of a real one
                                    brought tears to my eyes
Reality's kicked in and where we wanted so much more
                                    we've achieved a lot less
The plans for our garden like Monty's are in a complete and utter mess
The wife's in tears, winter's on the way, and summer's all but gone
Now I just think gardeners world is full of bullshit and so is that Monty Don.

Poems / Explanations

Having spent most of my younger years in our council flat with a 'veranda' the size of a postage stamp, I find that gardening and even people with gardens are alien to my world. I have no knowledge, experience, or interest towards gardening. Luckily, I married someone who had a different background, loves gardening, and looks after our modest garden to this day. It always looks wonderful, for which I am eternally grateful. When I look at what's currently on TV, there is a dominance of 'activity' or 'hobby based' programmes almost intravenously fed to us on a daily basis; like cooking, baking, DIY, painting, and, of course, gardening. It's interesting to note that, without exception, this category of television appears to be targeted towards an audience who are already motivated and often have the resources to buy the right kind of equipment and the sufficient space required to carry out the tasks. My mum, like all of the other mums I knew in my world, had a handheld whisk to make the pancakes in our kitchen where two people was often one too many.

'Just Like Monty Don' came out of those kind of memories and is not designed to be particularly critical but look at the way people without the appropriate facilities still get drawn into the 'dream' and tend to fall short of their intentions. Also, I find it incredibly funny that however small the gardens, or even backyards are, there has been almost a universal tendency to create mini theme parks for their children with swings, playhouses and sandpit, often causing the removal of grass, or any other kind of foliage.

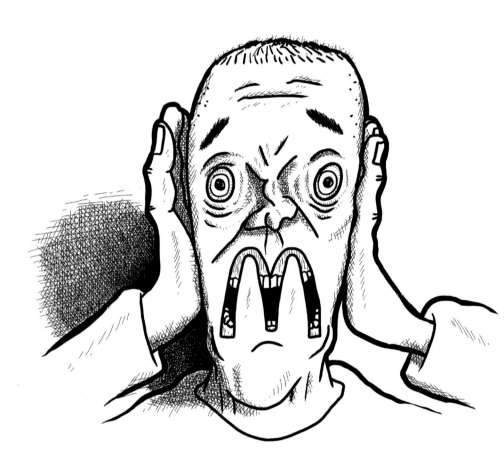

McDomination

Something which scares me that has crept across the nation
It's a modern day disease, a proverbial contamination,
Something that won't require much of an explanation:
It's Maccie D's invasion which will end in total McDomination!
Everywhere I look they're chopping down trees,
Creating more space to build more Maccie D's,
They already occupy the retail parks and still buying up land,
Maccies won't be content until they're fully in command.
We'll be summoned for our lunches, summoned for our teas,
There'll be special Maccie police to monitor consumption of Maccie D's.
Every street I walk down and every single corner that I turn,
That big yellow 'M' gives me great cause for concern,
McDomination isn't on its way because it's already here!
All the way down from McHope Street to the Mersey McPier,
There'll be no excuses accepted with Maccie D's fully on tap.
We'll all be given a 'Maccie ID' to log on to the Big Mac App,
There'll be targets to achieve with numbers of units to consume,
Failure to comply named and shamed on the 'Big Mac Zoom'.
We'll all be having Mcbreakfasts with our McCoffee or McTea,
McMarmalade on toast before we have our morning McPee,
They're buying up the world to gain total McDomination!
From London McEuston all the way up to McLime Street station.
Soon there'll be McSainsbury's, McAsda's and McTesco's on our streets.
We'll all be wearing McMaccie boots with McTrackers on our feet,
New franchises will appear like McWagamamas and McKFC's,
There'll be no escape from that big yellow 'M' or from Maccie D's,
So when I say that big yellow 'M' gives me reasons for concern,
You've been McWarned as we reach the McPoint of no return.

It is clear for all of us to see that despite the ongoing increase in clinical obesity around our country but particularly in children, that the government don't want to take on the responsibility of putting sufficient controls in place to prevent more and more junk food outlets getting planning permission to expand their empires. We all know that the type of processed foods these outlets sell are a complete and utter nutritional recipe for disaster, overloaded as they are with sugars, fats, and salts. The warning signs we've all seen over the past twenty years or more have now materialised into reality by causing high levels of diabetes and the inevitable associated side effects of high cholesterol and heart disease, which is a time bomb waiting to explode. Medical advice has been raining down on the government from top doctors and dietitians about the health issues directly linked to the consumption of this type of food and yet appear to have been largely ignored. 'McDomination' is a reflection of the growth of these outlets which has almost become a 'war for control' across the country between the various corporations competing for the business, and they're winning.

Poems / Explanations

I'M ALRIGHT JACK

Champagne and movies high in the sky,
Off to buy some bling in Milan or Dubai
More money than I can spend I cannot lie,
Yet the mothers in Africa squat in dust and cry
Several houses and cars, don't ask why,
Only ever in one place as much as I try
Extravagance beyond belief I can't justify,
While children in Africa lie waiting to die
I'm not clever, I'm not tall,
No good at spelling, but I can kick a ball
I'll cry like a baby should I need to fall,
It's one for the team it's more money for all
I'm a patron of some charity, not sure where,
Club said I need to 'show that I care'
Manager said it'd look good, don't need to be there,
Won't take much time maybe once a year
Well it's time to land, I can't wait to be there,
Got plenty of cash for my limousine fare
I've bought another new place, accountant said it's wise,
A great investment as prices will rise
My property portfolio is growing fast,
Don't worry about my future, don't think of my past
It does make me sad to think of African tears,
But I'm alright Jack, got no worries, got no fears.

I am a lifelong football supporter and still am a loyal true blue to my team Everton. Yet, like so many other people I speak to, I am utterly appalled at the money now involved at all levels of football and the eye watering numbers which are quoted during the transfer windows, particularly in the Premier League and the international markets across Europe and South America. The element of sport has been severely overshadowed, even diminished, by the sheer need (not desire) to win because of the financial rewards available through the various global broadcasting platforms and the marketing of the clubs as a brand. The 'wages' offered to the top players are ridiculous and, although I'm not a business owner, when the financial reports of the top clubs appear, the salary content is so high that a normal high street business could not and would not survive with those margins.

'I'm Alright Jack' is a take on those wage levels and the behaviour of some of the top footballers. It would be unfair to some of them as I am aware that some good charity work is carried out, but I do feel that they are often guided by image mentors to help raise their profiles. These guys are footballers, they are not highly-trained surgeons or ground-breaking scientists. Our schools are full of kids with enough potential to reach the very top in the sport. Messi and Ronaldo, as brilliant as they are, are certainly not in the irreplaceable category as so many people seem to think. Just saying.

A Day In A Minute

Wake up. Bad night
Fuse gone. No light
Shine me torch. Ooh, that's bright!
Down dog. Don't bite.
Let him out. Needs a shite.
Tea, toast... with marmite
Windy day. I'll fly me kite.
Phone call. Uptight.
Plans change. Big fright.
Time frame: too tight!
They're never wrong. Can't be right.
Disagree. Don't fight.
Quick lunch. Light bite.
Laptop. Report to write.
Be in by six tonight.
Heatings off. Fahrenheit.
Fleecy on. Frostbite.
Nearly done? Not quite.
Oh, fucked it up. Re-write!
Down dog. Don't bite.
Needs a walk. Oh, alright.
Day gone. Nearly night
Didn't get to fly me kite
Missed the pub. Hindsight.
Hit the pillow. Sleep tight.
Close me eyes. Night night.

Poems / Explanations

So many people say 'cherish every minute of every day' and I wholeheartedly agree with that sentiment. In fact, the older I get, the more it seems appropriate to do so. With this short piece I initially thought what if I could 'write a day in a minute', which is how it started out. The more thought I gave to it, the more I realised how many days in my previous working life have been absolutely ruined due to demands from other people, predominantly work related. Since the covid lockdown, more and more people have taken the 'golden opportunity' to work from home presumably thinking that being based at home is some kind of working utopia. Having been based at home with my sales related career over a 40-year span, I can assure those who are bothering to read this that it certainly is not the case. There are far too many distractions, from the coffee pot and biscuit tin to pets to children. The self-discipline required to knuckle down and get the job in hand done usually loses to the thought that 'I'll leave it 'til later, I've got all day'. The result usually leaves you burning the midnight oil as you try to catch up with the work you hadn't got done during the day.

My 'Day in a Minute' is therefore a combination of reflecting on one of those planned days off or when you think: 'well, if I can get finished I'll have a couple of hours to do whatever.'

Here's the thing: working from home, coupled with modern technology, makes you so much more accessible and tends to create a working relationship where the powers that be think, 'well he/she won't mind if I ask him/her to do this', 'it shouldn't take him/her long to complete this'. When, in actual fact, there is absolutely no consideration whatsoever for your personal agenda or state of mind, and the end result is often reflected in working longer hours and even more stress!

Poems / Explanations

Burnout

'I need it today', 'at the latest tomorrow'...
That's the mantra, beg steal or borrow,
Powerpoint, spreadsheets, Microsoft Excel,
Lost in this quagmire, delivered from hell,
Hotel bars and big shiny cars,
Clocking up a mileage from here to Mars,
Travel alone, sleep alone,
Talk to the kids from the end of your phone,
Laptops and iPhones are the new ball and chain.
You answer, you respond, but you'll never complain,
The crack of the whip is replaced by a digital ding
Whatever the request, you know it'll sting.
Close your eyes to get some sleep
To be woken with a ding or that digital bleep.
Shut up, piss off, just go away!
My nine to five has morphed into 24 a day,
The workload is relentless there seems to be no end.
At some point in time your mind has to bend,
That field of positivity you once owned and ran through
Can change so rapidly to a 'no can do'.
I must confess, my head's a mess,
I don't want this, I need a lot less.
Doctor, please tell me, are these chemicals ok?
Walking the floor all night, sleeping the rest of the day.
The emails have stopped and the digital dings have flown away.
No longer a queue in my in or my out tray,
The car will be next, and so will the pay.
I've been filed under useless, discarded and thrown away.

'Burnout' is about something so many people sadly face today, as indeed I faced it about 10 years ago. It's about people pushed to the absolute extreme by work, its demands, and the fake and toxic cultures that people find themselves in. It's about reaching a point where you cannot see either a way forward or a sensible and acceptable way out. It's about the pressures caused by so many changes in our working lives where modern technology is so unforgiving. There is no hiding place for so many because of the 'trickle down' culture of accountability to the point where if anything goes wrong then it must be your fault. You haven't got enough time in the day to complete the workload, so they'll send you on a 'time management course', which will not reduce the workload. They are run by external people who have no idea about the industry you work in and the relative issues which you have to overcome. BUT they've 'helped you' and now that they have 'given you the relative tools to do the job', any shortfall from now on will be YOUR FAULT!

Poems / Explanations

Communities need unity, because unity is good,
Unity gives opportunity, and opportunities are good.
Unity brings harmony, a state of being one.
Communities in agreement, or never far from,
Communities don't bear grudges, communities forgive.
Communities offer support, they live and let live.
Communities are open, and don't hide the truth.
Communities celebrate all from every pensioner to every youth.
When unity is unbroken, communities stay strong,
A message unspoken, a true place to belong.
Unity means sharing, more give and less take.
Communities are caring, communities don't make.
Communities are a fortress, they create an unbreakable bond.
Communities are streetwise, and refuse to be conned.
So, let's give our communities, the respect that we all should.
Community means unity, there's no space for bad blood.

This poem came about from an open mic event in Leigh, Lancashire, where they set a specific topic for all participants to write about. When 'community' was given, I really had to scratch my head and think a little bit before putting pen to paper. Although I fully accept not everything in the past was good, I did cast my memory back to when I lived with my nan and grandad until I was about 6 or 7.

We lived on a council estate, and I can recall that most people in the grove left their front doors open all day. There was a lot of communication between the neighbours. If I was sent to 'Mrs Jones' to take a message, the door would be open, and I could just walk in and inevitably would be offered a biscuit or a slice of homemade cake and made to feel welcome. These were pre-television days and I remember at weekends that neighbours would come into our house and play cards for entertainment.

This all sounds very nostalgic, and not everyone was always friendly. Yet there was always a great deal of mutual support in times of need, considering there was not a great deal of money around at the time and communities like this were commonplace. The re-distribution of people into high rise flats served only to break up communities like these and so my poem reflects how I would want my community to look like.

Poems / Explanations

EVERYTHING IS SO COMPLICATED

As I look through life's modern day prism,
Everything is sexist, racist or some kind of 'ism'
Nothing is simple anymore, way too much scrutiny
Causing chasmic social division and even some mutiny.
Recent revelations have totally exposed me,
I believed my life so far to be completely 'ism' free
But I've been found guilty through modern day causes,
Caught laughing out loud at *Only Fools and Horses*.
My 'fez' will have to go, no longer can be worn,
Tommy's top prop, now left forlorn.
Laughter has been banned, so my red nose is out,
In case it should offend sufferers of a condition known as gout.
Think of all those statues Ant and Dec have collected,
Twenty years on the run their public have selected,
Surely now they should all be taken away
Unless drink driving, drugs and wife dumping are now socially OK.
All impersonators need a quick change of career,
Allegedly only ever causing a constant river of tears
Sorry all you jocks, sorry all you taffs,
There'll be no tartan socks, and no yellow daffs.
So it's off to the charity shop with all of my favourite props
They'll serve no further purpose because of the PC cops.
The kilt has to go, the ginger wig too,
Those funny false teeth, that make me look like you.
Now I'm in fear of the prosecution powers,
My other guilty pleasure, a series called *Fawlty Towers*.
The DVDs are banned, can no longer stream it to view,
Nothing much left to watch, so I'll leave that thought with you.

Poems / Explanations

I'm a great believer of honesty and transparency, or 'having the cards on the table' as some people may put it, because the truth is the only platform from where real progress can be made in life, regardless of the situation. Any barrister has to dig deep to uncover any piece of evidence, regardless of how uncomfortable it may be, in order to guide the jury to make a fair and balanced decision. It's also impossible to plan where you're going if you cannot look back and trace the footsteps which have taken you to where you currently are. It's only learning from our past experiences, good or bad, that we can begin to shape our future for the better. It baffles me why some people think it's a good idea to erase parts of our history, especially comedy in theatre, tv, and film. The very basis of comedy as we have come to know it dates back to the late 15th century where commedia dell'arte began by defining characters split into three main groups of 'masters', 'lovers' and 'servants'. It later developed Into the 'stupid one', the 'smart one', the 'dominant one', the 'subservient one' and so on which can be traced throughout comedy from as far back as Shakespeare's Falstaff, through to silent movies such as Laurel and Hardy, right up to this day with the characters in our TV sitcoms, from Baldrick to Basil Fawlty and Manuel.

A lot of comedy has been based upon slapstick type of humour and other forms of humiliation which generally make fun of others. It's how life works. 'Everything is so complicated' is really based around that scenario where certain programmes from the past have now been made unavailable, censored or even part re-written to fit a certain narrative. My belief is that, by doing that, we would be depriving our youth of today and tomorrow of these important historical developments in comedy.

Poems / Explanations

Mal Bibby

PEOPLE DON'T LIKE CHANGE

It's hard to believe, in fact, it's quite strange
Generally speaking, people don't like change.
Change is inevitable, and change can be good,
But just because we can, does it mean that we should?
We can change where we live, change what we drive,
Change our destination, the time we choose to arrive.
Changes affect all of us in so many different ways
From train cancellations to airport delays.
We change our clothes with a change in the weather,
From sandals and t-shirts to woolly hats and leather.
We can change our reactions towards pleasure or fear,
Change our expressions, from joy through to tears.
We change what we eat, we change what we drink.
We can change our attitude and the way that we think.
We change what we look at on our big TV,
From Sky to Netflix to our crumbling BBC.
We change the way we look from our head to our toes,
The colour of our hair to the shape of our nose.
We change our socks and we change our shoes.
We change what we listen to from soul through to blues.
So it's still hard to believe because it sounds so strange,
That generally speaking, people don't like change.
Change can be brutal yet change can be kind,
Decisions are taken, then we change our mind...

Poems / Explanations

Mal Bibby

When any large changes are imminent in our lives, they are generally met with resistance or even severe opposition. Changes, if they are for the right reasons, can offer genuine benefits and should be embraced. However, people like to be surrounded by familiarity.

When things have been in place for many years, people feel comfortable and 'in control'. This poem is a cynical look at all of the things we do in everyday lives involving change. It's about those decisions we take for granted and probably don't even have to put much thought into. I found it quite funny that our lives often revolve around making decisions, whether to go 'left or right', 'up or down', 'early or late', 'blue or red' or whatever, yet when we're faced with any seismic changes we seem to stumble.

And as time goes on, I'm stumbling more often.

THE OLD GUY

He realises life is a circle and his is nearly complete,
His quest for honesty often drowned in a sea of deceit,
He's the old guy in the corner whose probably seen it all,
His opinion doesn't count, he's no longer on call,
He's the analogue passenger on a digital train,
A blast from the past with an old school brain,
Looked down on by many as a washed up pretender,
No influence left, no serious contender,
Naturally excluded from the inclusive dream,
He holds no currency, with nothing to redeem,
Still deals in cash, he bears no debts.
He's not well off, but carries no regrets,
He abides by the law, he sticks to the rules,
Won't tolerate lies, doesn't suffer fools.
He's no time for lifestyles which don't respect health,
He sees right through those who relentlessly chase wealth,
He holds knowledge and information in a bottomless well.
He's the old guy in the corner with more than plenty to tell,
Just one spark of interest and his eyes will glisten,
He'll grasp any chance to talk to anyone who'll listen,
Unexpected revelations which may sound too tall.
He's the old guy in the corner and he's definitely seen it all,
He's experienced plenty of life, taken a few chances,
His time so far, has exposed more questions than answers.
He trusts fewer now than he did long ago,
He's only the old guy in the corner, so what will he know?

The Old Guy came from me listening to an interview with a social care worker who was taking out an old lady for her weekly shopping.

As they drove, her radio was blurting out a Bob Dylan song and the care worker apologised to the old lady, who responded by saying 'It's fine. I like him. I know him very well...'

WHAAAAT?

Turns out she worked in the sixties for Dylan's record company in London and she was given the task of 'taking care' of Bob when he first came to England. Dylan apparently really liked this woman and rapidly built a strong rapport and insisted on any of his future visits to the UK that she was to be the one to look after him. Bob has continued to write and send cards to this woman for birthdays and Christmas ever since.

This in turn got me thinking that we have all, at one point in our lives, been in a bar or coffee shop and witnessed an elderly solo person staring into their glass or cup and we usually just move on without saying as much as a hello.

Wouldn't it be nice if we communicated more often? Everyone has a story to tell.

Poems / Explanations

MY FAMILY TREE

Like a never-ending soap that no-one could possibly write,
Disagreement and arguments inevitably ending up in a fight,
If only the truth, could rise to the top,
Who's really at fault, when will it stop?
If they're not talking to me and he's not talking to you,
It becomes increasingly difficult to know who's talking to who,
Mixed and twisted messages, he said, she said.
Assumptions made, opinions mislead,
So many relatives have been lost along the way,
Weddings and funerals, who is she? Who are they?
They'll stand around gulping free beer and pies,
With theatrical smiles shading the truth with their lies.
Where's Billy? Oh he's on holiday but he's doing fine,
When he's banged up again at Hornby Road Liverpool 9.
Where's Our Ginny? Oh she couldn't come because she's not well.
She must be back in the drying out unit, but you daren't ring that bell.
Church on a Sunday, but never ask why.
Bible thumping hypocrites who prefer to comply,
Desperate for recognition under a halo of deceit,
Believing prayers on a Sunday will make them complete,
This wholesome existence will lead them to the light,
Truth and honesty conveniently swept out of sight.
So there you have it, a snapshot of my family tree.
Some of the reasons I couldn't buy into their Christianity,
It's purely observational, that, I'm sure you can see,
Is the reason I prefer to focus, on what works for me.

My father's side of the family (though I totally exclude my father here) were evangelical born again Christians, which was something I grew up to increasingly loathe as time went by.

I have absolutely no problem with people finding comfort from whichever religion they may choose but I have a distinct dislike for the hypocrisy that I witnessed within my own family.

Everything was 'brushed under the carpet' for want of a better explanation. It was these ongoing events, over many years, which completely turned me away from organised religion of any kind, so much so that we never bothered to get either of our two children christened.

Poems / Explanations

FOUR SMALL ROOMS

Looking around and walking through the door
With a strange kind of feeling of not belonging anymore,
Faded recollections of happiness and fears
Distant memories of both laughter and tears,
Four small rooms with no privacy spared
Everything communal, everything shared,
Set amongst a community with inquisitive minds
Curtains always twitching, peeping through blinds,
Everybody looks when the new telly's arriving
Talk of the town, the loose tongues start jiving
Shed's get broken into, bikes go missing,
Curtain twitchers are silent, 'cos no-ones admitting
Arguments on the landing, usually about noise.
Limited access, prams and discarded toys
Doorbells not working, milk constantly nicked
Windows smashed when the first ball's kicked
Four small rooms up two flights of stairs
A place I called home for so many years,
Now empty, no life, everything laid bare
The end of an era, little left to share
It's Oxfam with the clothes and furniture to the tip
A lifetime of possessions destined for the skip
But nothings changed, it's the same old state of mind
Curtains are still twitching, they're still peeping thro' blinds.

I was raised in a loving family, by my mum and dad, in a council flat where I lived until I got married and moved into my own place with my wife. Both of my parents lived there until their death. They worked hard but never really had any money to speak of. My mum died first in 2002 and my dad only lasted six years after.

I hope the poem is deeper than it first appears, reflecting on the type of community where I had been raised and where my parents both lived out their lives. It looks back at the mentality of most of the neighbours, their often-petty attitudes over trivial matters, and how those memories come flooding back when the time came for me, as an only child, to empty the property.

It also touches upon how little they achieved in their lives and apart from me and my immediate family, how relatively unimportant their passing meant to most. It was a very emotional poem to write and still to this day is quite difficult for me to perform.

Poems / Explanations

THE WASPS NEST

Fifteen deluded narcissists, on national TV
Thank you Lord Sugar, for the opportunity,
For providing the platform to make such a fool out of me.
You were so fuckin' good, you didn't make week three,
Task after task, designed and set up to fail.
Drop your mates in the shit while you wag your tail,
Did you ever think so many pricks could fit under one roof?
Check out The Apprentice, and there's your proof
This weekly humiliation, Sugar's prime time slot,
Dressed up as entertainment, just to fund his yacht.
As the world looks and laughs he cares not one jot,
Luckily for the narcissists, it's all about their image,
Women struttin' their stuff, with bleached teeth and hair,
Men struttin' their stuff, with bleached teeth and hair.
There appears to be little requirement for brains or logic,
They're busy playing mind games like diagnosed psychotics,
Ooh Karen look at me! Ooh Lord Sugar look at me!
Maybe another missed diagnosis of ADHD?
These budding little entrepreneurs with ego's so big,
Make finding solutions look like an archaeological dig.
Always pointing the finger claiming others to blame,
For the predictable mega cockups it's the same old same
When you put your application in you thought you were so clever,
As one of fourteen losers, you'll be branded forever,
A proven failure exposed on national TV,
Yet you still believe you're the best Sugar will see.

I have never liked or even bothered to watch some of the absolute dross described as 'Reality TV' such as Big Brother and Love Island. Although I will admit to having watched The Jungle in its earliest form but that has predictably waned. This poem, however, is about the Lord Sugar panto called The Apprentice. I find it incredibly sad that the contestants who do get through to the programme really believe that it is all about them. They are of only comedic value, cheaply bought over by being accommodated in a ridiculously lavish and over-the-top mansion and being ferried about in a fleet of 'executive taxis' thinking they've 'made it'.

The reality is that the programme is all about Sugar and his constant need to have his ego polished on national television, alongside gaining God knows how much revenue towards his already overgrown fortune. These contestants are often exposed to be as thick as two short planks when given tasks to solve and the whole programme revolves around their failures and the humiliation associated with failing. They are also encouraged to goad each other and kick each other's butts in order to 'win'. What a nauseating spectacle the whole thing is!

Poems / Explanations

A Tory Sea Shanty

Hospitals are crumbling, and so are the schools.
There's not a penny to spare, said the Joker to the Fools,
Utilities would love to stop all the leaks, but they can't afford the tools,
So they continue to charge us more and fill our rivers up with stools

A government of pricks rotten to the core,
Policies of giving less but forever taking more,
Their attitude can only be described as simply savage,
Short-term thinkers, causing long-term damage.

'Milk the coffers dry boys, let's milk those coffers dry!
Walk right over the needy, and leave them there to cry!
Milk those coffers dry boys, oh milk those coffers dry!
Go fill our offshore bank accounts, 'til there's nothing left behind...'

Our once beloved golden egg has now collapsed into a mess,
There's only one thing left to privatise and it's not a difficult guess,
Reduce the services and gradually fund it less,
Let's make some more millions boys, let's sell off our NHS.

'Milk the coffers dry boys, let's milk those coffers dry!
Walk right over the needy, and leave them there to cry!
Milk those coffers dry boys, oh milk those coffers dry!
Go fill up our offshore bank accounts,'til there's nothing left behind...'

Largely self-explanatory, however, I have never witnessed a more corrupt administration than the current Tory government. We have now had to suffer over 13 years of their unnecessary 'austerity policies'. Cut back after cut back to council funding has resulted in a huge reduction in fundamental services to children, special needs, the elderly, education, as well as an almost complete breakdown of community and hospital medical access and availability, re-configuration of emergency fire services, closure of facilities like libraries, services such as refuse collection being run on a shoestring budget, dangerous hazards to motorists and pedestrians caused by the total abandonment of road and pavement maintenance and more. The list of their failures is almost as endless as the complete shysters promoted to the cabinet!

Poems / Explanations

MIND OVER MATTER

With a marketing qualification and a degree to go,
Little or no experience with the job in tow,
Making covert plans about where you should go,
Drip fed information on a 'need to know',
A pat on the back to ring your bell,
Looks of sincerity make it hard to tell,
Dare to return with no water from the well,
You were given the 'tools', it's your fault you fell,
With the inevitable inquest face to face,
Fingers will point straight to your case,
Justification required for why you failed to keep pace,
All validation rejected because you lost the race,
It's an old management technique of the Roman kind,
You'll be put to work you'll be made to grind,
Until there's nothing left then believe me you'll find,
That you really didn't matter, and they really didn't mind.

I think experience is often the best qualification anyone can have in most areas of life. If I needed a plumber to fit a new bathroom suite, I would want one who's been around the block a few times and not someone who has just read Part 1 of The Dummies Guide to Pipes. I have worked in quite a few companies in the corporate world, and it was quite common to see graduates come into the fold with little or no experience (other than the theory learned from books) and start calling the shots with suggestions which have already been tried and failed abysmally in the past. Naturally, such incompetence usually earns them quick promotion within the organisation.

'Mind over Matter' is partly written with that in mind but also how insignificant individuals really matter in the big picture within the corporate world. I have witnessed a flea collar salesperson rise to become a 'Global Director' in a very high-profile medical division, transported on a magic carpet fuelled by 5 star bullshit. Honestly.

Poems / Explanations

Mal Bibby

THE RED PEPPER AND CHILLI DIP BLUES

Please help me before I totally flip
Aldi have run out of my favourite red pepper and chilli dip
Morrisons and Tesco are way too dear
The Co-op and Lidl are nowhere near
In desperation I walk to my local corner shop
'Singhsbry's' can come in handy but his prices are over the top
He's got so many sauces on his shelf I don't know where to begin
From 'Rocky Mountain Buffalo' to 'Yung Lo Hoisin'
I'm searching through but I'm fast losing my grip
I can't find any of my favourite red pepper and chilli dip
My ready to eat chicken strips are now past their last day
So it's eat them now or simply throw them away
I haven't got the money to throw good food into a skip
I certainly can't face chicken strips without my favourite dip
My head is now spinning because I'm in an unsafe space
I can't be coping with no dip I'm in a really dark place
There must be others like me with the very same thought
Now I'm surfing the net to find some online support
Googles hit the spot as now I'm in chilli dip heaven
Endless lists of suppliers from Scotland through to Devon
But now I tumble from one fleeting moment of elation
To the darkest depths of no red pepper and chilli dip desperation
As I click on each supplier I'm left in total shock
Each and every one of them are completely out of stock
So to avoid disappointment of a supply chain apocalypse
Before you open up those ready to eat chicken strips
Take full heed of this vitally important tip
Make absolutely sure you've got your favourite dip!

It is laughable how we've all become accustomed to a huge range of choice in our supermarkets. We're all used to eat things in season, cheaply, and with a constant uninterrupted supply. We even expect seasonable fruit and vegetables to be fully available all year round, defying the very laws of Nature.

'Chilli Dip' was written when our shelves were showing large gaps in stock levels due (we were told) to the war in Ukraine and bad weather due to climate change affecting harvests in some countries. I'm not immune to feeling a bit selfish when I can't get hold of my favourite foods but it's a sign of how spoiled we have all become. I can imagine some well-heeled parent saying 'well I have to shop at Waitrose because my little Rupert won't eat his super spicy guacamole from anywhere else!'

I hope some day little Rupert will read this poem and know it's really all about him.

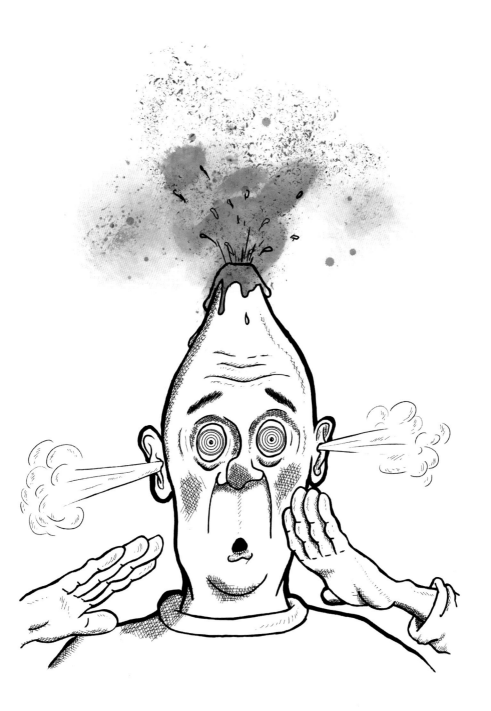

WHAT HAVE WE GOT?

We've got mass corruption in our government which seemingly never ends
Ministers on the take for their relatives and their friends
Billions syphoned away during the covid pandemic
Conveniently erased by the creators of the greed epidemic
We had Nightingale Hospitals built in weeks and never used
Millions upon millions wasted and budgets abused
This level of incompetence is there for us all to see

Yet these are the very same people who claim there is no ' money tree'
We've got a bunch of thugs in power with not one good intention
We've got teachers being held in permanent financial detention
We've got nurses and carers who don't even get a mention
We've got millions who can't survive on the standard state pension
We've got hospitals full up and can no longer offer a bed
We've got ambulance crews treating the dying and the dead
We've got members of staff who simply can't take any more
We've got waiting lists longer than we've ever witnessed before

We've got a police force and a legal system in complete dissarray
Headed up by people who have totally lost their way
Prisons are overflowing yet the serious bad boys are still at large
The best Khan can come up with is an extended congestion charge
We've got a broken social network and schools full to the brim
Crumbling medical provision where the predictions are grim
According to the gangsters in Westminster the futures looking bright
As a famous musician once said 'clowns to the left of me jokers to the right'

Poems / Explanations

These people in government have not got one iota of compassion. None of them ever have (or are highly unlikely to have) experienced need in their lives. They are totally focused on self and greed, as was clearly demonstrated during the Covid pandemic where so many opportunities were taken to benefit their own bank accounts. Hundreds of millions went 'missing' and have never been accounted for since. These overpaid administrators, many of them with large investment and property portfolios, live the high life in London. Their attendance at major conferences are funded by sponsors with hotel bills, flights, meals, often with their wives or partners, fully covered to eye watering amounts. They are the recipients of fully funded VIP hospitality packages to places like The Chelsea Flower Show, The Royal Opera House, and major sporting events. These same people are voting in parliament for a reduction in benefits for those in true need. They have no moral compass. They don't care. Shame on them.

Poems / Explanations

SELF-DESTRUCTION

Crypto currency, driverless cars
Recreational trips to far away stars,
The big money moguls are back on the make,
Silicon Valley has baked a brand new cake.
Artificial intelligence is not tomorrow, it's here today
As this volcano erupts it will pave its own way
AI is preparing to take control of the nation
Is this welcome relief, or permanent dislocation?
The technos are coming, robots are on the rise
Livelihoods threatened, jobs in demise
Artificial information won't be a passing trend
Microchips on steroids, your mind's about to bend
One sure way to gain compliance, is to instil sufficient fear.
Forget information in clouds, this is a brand new stratosphere
We are all sitting back and casually watching it unfold,
This real World War Three, to gain ultimate control
If you're goal is radicalisation, just ask AI.
If you want to rig the next election, just ask AI.
Technology has shrunk our world to a goldfish bowl
We've created the monster no-one can control
A digital Frankenstein on the brink of global release
The terrorists new playground. Every scammers feast
From the smallest little beehive, AI will take all the honey,
From the biggest global bank, AI will control that money
Whenever you're faced with choice, AI will make that decision
Delivered with the accuracy and speed of a surgical incision
AI is the future and it's here today
Neither you nor I can stand in its way
For the privileged few this will be their digital utopia
For the rest of us it will become our nightmare dystopia.

I have never been a 'technophobe'. Being of a certain age when I was first introduced to computing, I found the speed and capacity of PCs frightening. Yet evolution is inevitable and just like machinery replaced cottage industries during the Industrial Revolution, and cars replaced horses, computers have been driving our lives for several decades now. There is no doubt that many good things have emerged, usually under the guise of 'efficiency'. The power of technology has been constantly emphasised by the different platforms which have become available together with the ease of access on to the information superhighway. Social media has demonstrated time and again how influential online activity can be for individuals wishing to lift their profile for whatever purpose they may choose. Large corporations are using social media for sales and marketing campaigns, government departments have maximised the 'dot com' world to support their 'self-help' sites from taxation to benefits to passports and just about everything else. Political parties, social groups and activists are all fully on board with this technology which has now become a 'must have'. Like it or not, this level of activity and data collection has led our lives in a direction where our profiles are all now defined by some algorithm. We are processed, filtered, and placed into convenient boxes. I believe my fears have been justified.

AI is now the new technological 'advancement' and is on a completely different level to anything we have so far experienced. A.I. is on a par with discovering a new planet, and while still in its infancy, we know only too well that speedy developments will occur in this field and so I am fearful yet again. The ability of A.I. to mimic, its ability to reason and make decisions, and to be able to produce written work on any subject in seconds worries me. Of course, there will be benefits to gain from A.I. but I think it can only give more opportunities to the dark side of the cyber world, hence 'Self-Destruction'.

Poems / Explanations

WALK DOWN ANY STREET

Walk down any street , you're sure to find drugs.
You'll step over homeless, you'll avoid mindless thugs.
24/7, as day turns to night,
Where did it go wrong, or where did it go right?
Short-term partners, no more wives,
Wild-west guns, eastern knives.
Check your bank, in case you've been scammed,
Is there any way back, are we forever damned?
Look in the mirror, avoid 'crash for cash',
Too many drivers, driving way too fast,
Banned with no insurance, not even taxed.
Don't shake your head, they are the facts,
We've created a society, that no longer cares,
Jump the queues, dodge the fares.
Don't point the finger, we're all to blame.
The world's gone soft, laws have gone lame,
What will it take, to put things right?
Can we ever recover, from such a venomous bite?
Are we all just too busy to ever turn it round?
Riding our very own selfish merry-go-round?

More of the intractable problems of modern living. We are all to blame for the chasmic drop in standards, the lack of respect we have towards each other.

Tolerance is a real virtue to have but I believe that our attitude towards 'anything goes' has really backfired as society descends into increasingly feral behaviour. The powers-that-be have failed abysmally to control or even contain the mobilisation and distribution of illegal drugs across the nation which has contributed to the ongoing growth of an industry which can only be described as evil. Driven and controlled by the money lords and completely at the expense of all of those at the lower end of the food chain causing an increase in dependency, more crime and violence between 'street gangs', and general overall misery.

Our governments have failed to come to terms with the homeless situation throughout our cities and the evidence is there for all to see. The numbers of homeless are increasing significantly and yet very little appears to be done about it or even spoken about at a political level.

Just Saying...

There's litter in the parks and litter on the streets
Broken bottles in doorways, empty Maccies at my feet
Ingrained in the pavements are ciggie butts and gum
Makes me shake with anger, makes my senses feel numb
Ignorance and arrogance has never been good
Just what are we dealing with under those hoods?
Spitting saliva they think they look cool
Acting like clowns and looking like fools
Polite signs everywhere begging us to refrain
There's still litter on buses there's still litter on trains
Feet on seats, headphones on nine
Smoking and laughing at the threat of a fine
Pollution in the skies, rivers full of shite
Let's go trash our streets every day and every night
This feral behaviour has become the norm
Showing disrespect and in need of reform
Half-eaten burgers, ketchup and chips
A tsunami of rubbish, an urban Apocalypse
Banana milkshakes left standing in their cup
Next to a pool of 'carrots' that someone's thrown up
Well I've said all I need to say, so now I'll calm down
There's just one thing left, anyone coming to town?

The content of this poem doesn't warrant a fully blown explanation, but there are a few observations I'd like to make here. Years ago, when Brits began to flood Europe on holidays, it was largely accepted that many of these holiday destinations which were visited had a rather tainted image of their 'cleanliness' as compared to Britain. How laughable is that now!

I am fortunate enough to have travelled a little and, for example, if you take Barcelona as one of the most visited cities in Spain, you will see street cleaning vehicles operating in the city centre up to midnight including the weekends. The trains on the Metro are also kept very tidy, and this level of cleanliness can be seen across many of the cities I have visited in Europe. I don't see that in the UK, in fact I see the opposite, and I cannot imagine what foreign visitors think of this country when they arrive here. Firstly, there are the relentless levels of so-called 'austerity' by this government where ongoing cutbacks in funding have forced local authorities to make unfortunate and unpopular decisions, and secondly, the appalling drop in respect across the nation where throwing litter onto our streets has apparently become socially acceptable, which I find incredibly sad.

Poems / Explanations

A SELF DIAGNOSIS

Queues at takeaways across the whole of the nation
Caused apparently by 'chronic appetite dysregulation'
A condition with which I'm unfamiliar but need to find out
To check if it could possibly exacerbate my diabetes and gout
It's a common problem and as yet with no known cure
Where enough isn't enough, still craving for more
I suffer with those symptoms and so I need more information
Because I know I've developed this 'chronic appetite dysregulation'
My dietitian wants me to control my intake of food
That's difficult being one click away from Deliveroo
Chicken nuggets with extra sides and dips
2 for one go large with the chips
The medics have told me my health's at risk if I don't cut back
Maybe just the one milkshake then, with that double 'Big Mac'.
I tried to convince them at my last consultation
It's not the food and drink it's this 'chronic appetite dysregulation'
Of course ever increasing prices are beginning to take its toll
I've made a couple of little tweeks to keep my costs under control
I've scrapped my Thursday takeaway from the 'Rising Moon'
Replaced it with half price curry night at our local Weatherspoon
Our chippy's closed down because of the price of fish
I'm now on the lookout for an alternative equally nutritious Friday night dish
My blood pressures up again so I'll probably need further medication
I know it's not the food, it's definitely this 'chronic appetite dysregulation'
Doctor told me that exercise would be really good for me
So I've even started walking to Dominoes and KFC
Doc was banging on about 10,000 steps or more
I've measured, it's 1250 steps, door to door
So now I can cut my visits to KFC from 5 days a week to 4.
Hit my target, reduce my spending, and save even more,
Every hospital visit I have to endure the same old nutritional interrogation
I tell them it's not the food and drink it's 'chronic appetite dysregulation'
Doc says if i don't lose any weight my future won't look so bright
I've already reduced my beer intake from 5 to 4 pints a night

Poems / Explanations

Mal Bibby

I've cut out crisps, chocolate snacks, my favourite Liquorice and sherbet dab,
Now their moaning about my once a week Saturday night donner kebab
The clinic now want to 'help me' to make a brand new start,
They've given me a'daily food and liquid consumption chart'
I can't for the life of me think what good that could possibly do
There's only one tiny box to write in so entries may not be factually true
For example on a Thursday after my Weatherspoon half price curry
I usually nip in to 'Maccies' to wash it down with a vanilla McFlurry
So if i can't fit it all in that little box there may be some misrepresentation
But the food's not the problem it's the 'chronic appetite dysregulation'
My next appointment at the hospital is 10 'o'clock tomorrow with the doc
Which means i'll have to delay my morning fry-up 'ti after eleven 'o'clock
That's a logistical nightmare for me because it's so close to lunch
The cafe will have stopped breakfasts so I'll have a Weatherspoon's brunch
I told them to shove their 'daily food and liquid chart', which didn't go well
They discharged me from the clinic, wished me good luck & farewell
They did emphasise that my self diagnosis was all in my imagination
As there is no known medical condition called 'chronic appetite dysregulation'

Poems / Explanations

When I went to secondary school it was very strictly run as it was during the early sixties. Not everything in those days was perfect by any stretch of the imagination but there was an unspoken respect for the pecking order from the younger boys up to the older ones and of course it was mandatory to respect the teachers, but political correctness had not yet been invented. I remember many times when we were lined up in the yard or the playing fields and one of the teachers would yell 'YOU!'

'Who? Me sir?'

'NO! The ginger boy next to the fat one on the end.'

Today that would be unheard of but nobody got hurt. It was just part of the huge learning curve during the transition from boy to young man, it was just called Life and none of us considered ourselves to be a victim as such, we just got on with it.

The scrutiny which is now applied daily to every word we use to communicate with each other on whatever platform, either verbally face to face or via social media is absolutely mind boggling. It is so simple to unpick the content of any dialogue and reduce the response to 'what do you mean by that?' and causing an untold number of confrontations between people. Add to that the ever increasing 'blame culture' where personal accountability appears to have faded beyond redemption and there is always someone or something else to be the cause of the 'problem' And that's where we are today. 'A Self Diagnosis' is based around how we have started to soften and dilute our terminology to accommodate these changes in attitude.

BY DEFINITION

Words are often interpreted in so many different ways
An insignificant little fire, conveyed as a life threatening blaze
Our individual perceptions differ and are unlikely to be the same
Words are so powerful they can change allegation into blame
Definitions should be short and very concise
Giving explanations which are clinically precise
Descriptions designed so we all fully understand
Delivering the clarity required with no need to expand.
What people say doesn't always convey what they mean
Carefully chosen dialogue often used as a screen
An area where politicians have outstanding expertise
Every tory minister seems to be infected with this verbal disease
You or I would be branded as 'careless' should we spill our coffee
What a different meaning this holds for Nadhim Zahawi
Apparently being 'careless' now includes offshore investments
A kind of money laundering to avoid income tax assessments.
This arrogant piece of pond life treated everyone around him as fools
He took it upon himself to apply his own homespun taxation rules
Yet another Tory millionaire who has redefined the term greed
One who will never understand or suffer the humiliation of need
Who cares that your cloak of authority is no longer approved
You lied to the bitter end until it was forcefully removed
Mr Zahawi shame on you, by definition you are a cheat and a liar,
In your world no life threatening blaze, just an insignificant little fire.

'By Definition' came about when Nadhim Zahawi, then a high-flying, high-profile Tory Minister with a succession of posts in the government, had been questioned by HMRC about his involvement in an offshore investment fund from as far back as 2020 and his failure to submit the relevant paperwork. This was a clear attempt to avoid taxation and was recognised as a 'serious breach' of the ministerial code over his own tax affairs, for which he was subsequently sacked from his ministerial post, as well as Chair of the Conservative Party. He was also fined for a non-payment of capital gains tax on shares allegedly worth £27m (which in turn should have been taxed at around £3.4m). This was almost laughable having previously been the Chancellor of the Exchequer from July 2022 to September 2022 and then Minister for Equalities until October 2022, making the whole episode an utter disgrace for himself and the government.

Zahawi had made a strong case for himself and his family for 'rising from nothing' as an immigrant from Iraq who had worked hard and made a good life in Britain and who is now giving a solid contribution back to society which has been so kind to him. Well isn't that nice? When it turns out that he's just another Tory thug hiding under a false cloak of decency with criminal tendencies to avoid taxation or use their position in government to line their own pockets. These people are running our country, and they are the most corrupt, greedy and self-serving group of people I have ever come across in my life.

Poems / Explanations

A SIMPLE PUB LUNCH

While it's heaven for many, some consider it banal,
For me nothing beats that quiet pub right by the canal.
Sun streaming down watching the ducks float by,
Carpets of wild flowers under a clear blue sky.
As the ice cold beer starts to tease the appetite,
It's time for lunch that all important bite.
This is a gastro pub so the food ain't cheap here,
Keep it simple just a sandwich to accompany the beer.
While reading the menu I hear a pleasant friendly voice
'Good afternoon sir. Have you made your choice?'
I'm really struggling as they all sound so very nice
I'd value your guidance and maybe some advice.
'No worries let's get started and open up your tab
How about our responsibly sourced sustainable crab?'
I'm on limited time so looking at the one which will come sooner
But I am tempted by the sound of that dolphin friendly yellow fin tuna.
'Don't worry when the orders are placed service is fast,' he said
I'm not really keen on crab so I'll choose another instead.
'How about our farmers' market brie with spiced Moroccan apricot jam?
Or a bed of home pickled coleslaw with locally sourced oak smoked ham?'
Well the ham's out as I'm pescatarian, so I don't eat meat
The brie may trigger traumatic memories of my old nanna's feet
If I had more time I'd choose the traditional Bengalese vegetarian bhuna
But I must move soon so I'll settle for the dolphin friendly yellow fin tuna...
'Excellent choice, would that be a wrap, open sandwich or
freshly baked baguette?
Let's have the open sandwich with optional salad and croquettes.
'We have a wide selection of breads either brown or white
Wholemeal, multigrain, rye, sourdough light...'
My dietitian has recommended that I eat gluten free.
'I'll check with the kitchen sir. I'll just go and see.'
Please make sure when you have checked the bread
No butter. I require a gluten free spread.
'So that's one dolphin friendly yellow fin tuna on open gluten free bread

Poems / Explanations   59

With optional salad and croquettes with a gluten free spread?
Yes, thank you, now what dressing would you like?'
I don't really mind because I'm conscious of the time.
'Well with the tuna, I'd recommend the vegetarian low fat mayo
with chilli and lime.'
Ok, I'll go with that...
'So that's: one dolphin friendly yellow fin tuna on open gluten free bread with
optional salad and croquettes with gluten free spread and the vegetarian
low fat mayo with chilli and lime dressing
Yes, that'll be fine, would you like any sides?'
No thanks just the sandwich.
'Well because you've made a selection from our premium menu
You are entitled to any side for half price...'
Ok, I'll have some chips please
'Would that be our lightly seasoned organic handcut traditional chips, our air
fried sweet red potatoe skins, or our very popular curly french fries?'
I'll have air fried sweet red potatoe skins please. 'Regular, or large?'
Let's go large. 'There'll be a £1.00 surcharge for that sir.'
'Right, so that's one dolphin friendly yellow fin tuna on open gluten free
bread, with optional salad and croquettes, with gluten free spread and the
vegetarian low fat mayo with chilli and lime dressing and a large portion of air
fried sweet red potatoe skins...'
Yes. Thank you.
'Because you are now over £15.00. You qualify for a complimentary glass
from our excellent house wine selection,' he said.
'Italian pinot grigio white, or South African shiraz red?'
No thanks I'll stick with my beer, I just need to be fed.
Several minutes later
'I'm so sorry sir chef says there's no yellow fin tuna left so I've cancelled that
order.
Can we start again please?'

Poems / Explanations

Oh, my how things have changed over the years where pubs and food are concerned! Over 40 years ago, I was a sales rep, and one hot summer's day on the way home I decided to stop off for a pint. The pub was out in the sticks and empty when I walked in. Behind the bar was a huge guy who could easily have passed as a farmer with thick bushy hair and a ruddy red face. He asked what I would like, to which I replied, 'a pint of lager and could I please have a plain cheese or ham sandwich?' He looked at me, pulled the pint of beer and said, 'well what's it to be, ham or cheese'? I said cheese would be fine. About 5 minutes later he re-appeared with what I can only describe as a doorstep of a sandwich comprising of a block of cheese between two thick slices of white bread and placed it on the bar. How much is that I asked and to my amazement and confusion he shook his head and said, 'No it's ok' but I insisted on paying to which he replied, 'We don't do food here'.

Of course, since then pubs have developed and morphed into restaurants that serve drinks, but even more than that we have had the transformation from 'pubs with food' to 'gastro pubs' almost self-appointing themselves to a higher level in the mind of the customer where, through clever marketing, they have been able not only to increase the food side of the business but to ramp up profits by charging similar prices of some well-known high street restaurant chains. Couple this with the terminology now used in menus where all food appears to be 'only the very best handpicked', 'carefully selected by our own award-winning chef', 'organically grown vegetables' and so on, and we have all taken the bait. The choices available now and the ordering procedure always brings a smile to my face and I can't help but to recall my experience all those years ago which sparked 'A Simple Pub Lunch'.

Poems / Explanations

FEELING UNWELL

Getting from A to B is becoming a major problem for me,
I've got what's generally known as a chronically bad knee.
I've been limping in pain for a year or two you see,
But getting to see the doctor ain't what it used to be.
The nurse has been helpful full of good advice,
I've seen no evidence of a doctor in the building, but told they're all very nice.
I've been a supporter of the NHS almost since its inception,
The big challenge now is how to get past that reception.
There she sits behind the glass. Built like a Centurian tank.
If she was a piece of wood she'd be a 6 by 2 solid oak plank.
She's got a gritty determination to keep most patients out,
Her success rate is phenomenal the empty waiting room leaves no doubt.
She can pull a face which could be easily mistaken for a chewed up toffee
I've only ever seen her painting her nails or drinking her coffee.
She looks like Mount Vesuvius just waiting to erupt.
'No you can't see the doctor, he's busy!' Polite but abrupt,
This woman is programmed, she could stop the tide from coming in.
She's waterproof. Non-stick. She's an all-weather wheelie bin.
She shows no compassion for your discomfort or pain,
She'll deliberately keep you waiting as if buying a ticket for the train,
She's never remotely concerned about the ever growing queue,
Because all of a sudden she needs to know 'What's wrong with you?'
When I'm feeling unwell I believe it's time for a visit to the quack's,
I don't want a conversation at a window about dysfunctional bowels
                              or bad backs.
I thought receptionists were employed to dish out the appointment,
Not to deciide whether I need physiotherapy or a tube of ointment.
Requests for appointments are greeted with her signature laser beam stare,
You'd be more likely to be fully refunded from Easyjet or Ryanair.
You could easily be forgiven for thinking she really doesn't care,
But that short moment of control is so very important to her.
Looking at a screen, shaking her head, clearly enjoying the domination
A theatrical smile as she offers a week on Thursday for,
                              A telephone consultation

Mal Bibby

This piece offering is not what you wanted, she says it's 'the best she can do'.
Staring back with her poker face, the decision is now entirely down to you.
She'll consider this a success albeit she knows it didn't meet your expectation
You're now face to face with a consummate master of confrontation
With this single option on offer you nod in agreement with the
                                                chewed up toffee.
She's won, you've lost, she's back to painting nails and drinking coffee.
A week on Thursday arrives and as promised the phone rings at two
It's the doctor I've never met and he says 'what can I do for you?'
I explained my chronic mobility issues caused by my dodgy knee.
'Well I can't diagnose that on the phone, you'll have to come in and see me.'
But doc. I've tried the phone. The NHS app. And I've even tried online
I've limped up to the surgery and joined the queue, just to be declined
I don't know what it is that's keeping you busy doc and
                                                I don't want to sound rude,
I've got more chance of McCartney knocking on my door singing Hey Jude
'Well,' said the doc. 'I shouldn't really do this but if it's as bad as you say
I'll write directly to the hospital and refer you straight away.'
Now I'm on a waiting list which they inform me is at least 12 months long
So I've got a tenner on at Betfred on McCartney knocking and singing that
song.

Poems / Explanations

I, amongst many people, have been extremely fortunate to have had the luxury of free access to the NHS and its associated services throughout my life, and to date, whenever I have had to rely on them, they have been there to support me. This poem was born out of sheer frustration, which I'm sure you may have experienced yourself in more recent times. The ever-increasing number of mechanisms being put into place to prevent people from actually seeing a doctor are making life difficult for many patients.

'No appointments available, try ringing before 9 in the morning to get an emergency appointment...'

'Try advice from our website.'

'See if your local pharmacist can help or advise you.'

'Call 111.'

'Fill in an online form to be considered for an appointment.'

'Will a telephone consultation be acceptable?'

'Send in a digital photograph of the problem'.

Less than several years ago, none of the above was even heard of and would almost definitely have been rejected had patients been consulted over their introduction. It now appears to me that receptionists have become an integral part of these deliberately set hurdles to access within all of our health centres. I am sure that these issues are planned and directly related to the current government's desire to bring our NHS closer to privatisation.

Is It Just Me?

I've got an oven and hob that I hardly ever use
I've got a George Foreman grill with a dodgy fuse
I've got a pressure cooker I've never read the book
I've got an artisan food mixer, never read the book
I've got a popcorn maker and a chocolate fountain
Enough sugar to create a diabetic mountain
I've got a cup-cake maker and a candy-floss machine
Some earthenware thing to make a 'lamb tagine'
I've got a smoothie maker and a hand held whisk
I could throw a small party inside my casserole dish
I've got a special jug, to filter all my water
And an evil looking thing called a pestle and mortar
Got a Sodastream syphon to make my own pop
A milkshake maker like you see in the shop
I could create a vegan banquet with my salad shaker
Bake my own bread with my own bread maker
I've found mothers recipe books way back from Keith Floyd
A rack of Indian spices I'm sure I'd be wise to avoid
I've got Jamie Oliver pans, and my Rick Stein knives
A James Martin chopping block to chop up my chives
I'm watchin' Gino's Italy and Ramsey's Hell Kitchen
And that American shite where they never stop bitchin'
Well I've had enough of this cooking lark, not sure about you
But thankyou Mr Microwave and God Bless Deliveroo.

Mal Bibby

Last year my wife and I purchased an 'air fryer' based largely upon the spin from the media and advertising how much cheaper it would be to use to cook certain foods against the cost of using a traditional gas or electric oven, which with the recent upsurge in fuel bills seemed to make a lot of sense. Without going into too much detail, (because I think there is a good poem to be had about these) the actual marketplace for air fryers is unbelievably vast, so be very careful which one you choose if you are heading down that route. Most things we've attempted so far have either flopped, flipped, burnt, or stuck.

However, 'Is it Just Me?' was created because we didn't realise just how much space these items can take up, and when we started to look for a suitable storage area in the kitchen, we soon began to come across a lot of items which had been hiding at the back of the cupboards for some time, and in some cases for years. Based upon a stream of 'findings' the conversation went along the lines of 'what's this for', 'oh that's a lolly-ice maker, 'have we ever made any lolly-ices?' and so on. I'm sure you get the gist. The poem itself is a slightly exaggerated and humorous look at that scenario but it has been well received where I have performed it because people obviously relate to it. This in turn made me think of all of the different devices which have entered the marketplace and with the right level of advertising they've actually sold and even made some people into overnight millionaires: sandwich toasters that make your toastie look like a seashell; egg poachers to make the perfectly circular poached egg. Why?

A BROKEN SOCIETY

A broken society can only offer broken support
Go spend a day in any magistrates court
So many lost souls who've become enveloped in crime
Disengaged parents who've failed to invest time
A society where money has become the ultimate prize
Trained up in violence, de-sensitized
No limits or boundaries, nor visible lines to cross
Inflicting maximum damage to show who's the boss.

There'll be no negotiation, no time to talk
Just violent actions to prove who can walk the walk
Chances of being caught are virtually nil
There's nothing to fear so go for the kill
Dominance should not be defined with blood
How can we reverse something so bad, back to good
Idolising spoken word born out of aggression
Carving such a negative and indelible impression

This frayed society offers no path to recovery
It has no answers to sheer arrogance and effrontery
Knives and guns prove none of us are immortal
Check their availability on the dark web portal
Stop and search probation or prison
None of it works we need a fresh new vision
It's real and it's now, not for poems or plays
This broken society, needs alternative ways.

Mal Bibby

I am certain that all behavioural patterns of children are formed at home, and it is plain for all of us to see the way general standards of respect in our society have plummeted to unacceptable depths. The subject is way too deep for me to even think I am in some kind of position to offer solutions here as I am not, however, I can only reflect upon what I see around me on a daily basis, and as we stand right now, none of it appears to be working. When I look back at the explanation of my poem 'Community' where I lived with my grandparents until I was 6 or 7 and every neighbour's front door was left open during the daytime and make a direct comparison. Now that just doesn't happen. Communities have broken down and the cost of that is all around us. The sheer volume of criminal activity and violence going on around us in our own neighbourhoods every single day is colossal and, sadly, on the increase. The landscape has altered dramatically for social and political reasons, but the facts are there. We have morphed into a 'must have' society at all costs and the amount of drug dealing, shoplifting and online fraud have become the 'norm' for far too many to generate incomes.

Poems / Explanations

FROM DAD

Whenever you gave me a card it just always read 'from Dad'
I know you did really love me, from when I was a lad
I can recollect many good times, and very little bad
You couldn't hug me though, could you Dad?
The day I got married, I'll never understand
No congratulations, nor a shake of the hand
You came from a different time, but I still find it sad
You couldn't ever hug me, could you Dad?
The birth of both our children brought us all so much joy
First our precious daughter. Then our beautiful little boy
We all shared tears and laughter from good times we had
You couldn't hug me though, could you Dad?
The night mum died, I was lost for words to say
As I reached out with both arms you turned the other way
But I know deep down, you really did love this little lad
You just couldn't ever hug me, could you Dad?

This short poem is really about generational differences. It was never intended to be a criticism of my father, although it may appear that way to some on first reading. I cannot recollect my dad ever complaining about his upbringing, but I do know that as one of nine children (with four brothers and four sisters) and with a coal miner as their father, he was brought up in abject poverty and in the most extremely humble surroundings. My dad once shared with me that at Christmas time, they each received just a stocking with a tangerine, some nuts, and a small bar of chocolate. There would be no cards or 'main gifts' for any of them. That was it. Birthdays weren't celebrated apart from verbal 'Happy Birthdays' and certainly no cards or gifts for any of them. All of this was not uncommon in the lower tiers of society, and so it was very much of its time, and of course largely financially driven. It therefore came as no surprise to me that making any kind of an event out of birthdays and Christmas was totally alien to my dad and yet, throughout his entire life, he was one of the most generous people I could ever have wished to meet. If all he had was ten pounds in his pocket and you needed it more, he wouldn't hesitate or even think about it, it would be yours.

Compare those days with now, where recent generations are so much more tactile, openly hugging each other in the streets, the social media platforms are inundated with birthday wishes across the globe often to people they've met once on holiday, and the annual mad scramble at Christmas time where people risk going into heavy debt just to obtain the latest trendy gifts and technology. Some consider it to be progress, and where I would not suggest the 'good old days' were better, my point is how both gratitude and attitude have changed out of proportion.

Poems / Explanations

HAPPINESS

There's so much good in our lives but sometimes there's bad
Happiness will always, be balanced with sad
Happiness is here. For each and everyone to take
It comes from within, it's what each of us make
Happiness is free and something to be shared
With our smiles and laughter to show that you cared
Happiness can never be defined by what's on your plate
One man's good fortune, will be another man's fate
Would your happiness and my happiness be the same
If my horse could run, but yours was lame
Levels of happiness can be many worlds apart
Some are happy to walk while others crave fancy cars
If happiness is something you need to constantly chase
Your journey will be a long one my friend, you won't win that race
You'll make many an acquaintance with a similar frame of mind
Chasing that same pot of gold. Which neither are likely to find
Happiness is infectious, it lives in our hearts and our head
It's the healthiest of pandemics. That everyone should spread
So much easier to value the things you have already got
Than to chase in a race, to discover a worthless empty pot
The man with no teeth is still able to smile
Where the man without happiness can only spit bile
Happiness is not judgemental and is free from political hype
Wears no badge of gender, or of any other particular type
Happiness can't hide and it won't tell any lies
Happiness beams out through our laughter and our smiles
There are few valuable commodities in life which come for free
I'll be happy for you and live in hope that you'll be happy for me.

A very simple little poem mostly about the type of people who chase what really doesn't exist. Their constant need for more and more materialistic possessions in order to impress other people in their lives and their fundamental belief that they are more important than those who are not in a position or choose not to do the same. They treat life as some sort of 'pecking order' based upon money and power, and, where there is absolutely nothing wrong with ambition or achievement in life, to me it's more of an attitude and how, in the end, their individual successes and achievements are put to use. It's a lot more sensible and will bring more satisfaction to appreciate what you've got in this life than to chase a superficial dream.

Poems / Explanations

Mal Bibby

IT DIDN'T DO WHAT IT SAID ON THE TIN

How many products have you bought which end up in the bin?
Just because they didn't do, what it said on the tin
Why are companies allowed to lie, on a biblical scale
Exaggerating claims, about their products on sale
We all suck it up and rarely complain, as they scoop millions
                                        in profits - time and again
You don't need to look far, the markets are congested
Misleading adverts. Protecting their millions invested
We all buy into it because it's 'scientifically tested' they get away with it
                                        because no-one protested
'No added sugar', and do you want to know why?
They can't cram any more in, as much as they try
What about 'clinically proven' yoghurts, are they really the solution?
Supposed to help your guts and your morning ablutions
Too many of these and you know, you'll require medication to
                                        bung up the flow
A chocolate bar that helps you' work rest and play', no mention of
                                        type 2 diabetes or tooth decay
'Single coat paint' – well that's what they sold to the nation
I doubt that's been tested on student accommodation
One coat won't work on walls, which are cracked and peelin
You'll need a third tin, to cover the fungus on the ceiling
Energy drinks that 'Give You Wings', what a load of cock
Because if it did, it'd be like Quidditch round the Albert Dock
Someone's havin' a laugh, '72 hours protection because by Thursday
                                        you'll smell like a bad infection
Coercive language designed to persuade, fill a bottle up with sugar,
                                        you've got 'Glucozade'
Twisted information, claiming to boost our health
When their sole objective is to increase their wealth
Sugar free – fat free – what the hell's in that tin
Genetically modified powder with dayglo colours in
Next time you're shopping scrutinise that label
And sift out the facts from the corporate fable.

Poems / Explanations

One of my other poems 'Is it just me?' paints a picture of how gullible we all tend to be when certain items are invented and marketed and we all fall for the spin and end up buying things that really aren't needed, or at least, are not much of an improvement on what we already have. Almost like re-inventing the wheel as it were. 'It didn't do what it said on the tin' explores more of the outrageous claims often made by companies about the products they are advertising on all of the various media platforms from billboards, tv, radio, magazines, and more recently social media. Strong persuasive terminology used to create nothing more than a myth which they hope, and are so often right, that we will all believe. How many times have we seen the word 'magic' used in advertising, 'world beating', 'like nothing ever seen before'. The regular use of high-profile entertainers or sports people to endorse their products, very few of whom would be seen dead using the actual product but are still offered ridiculous sums of money to promote them. They will stop at nothing in order to convince us all that we would be bordering on stupid if we didn't fork out our hard-earned cash for their products. So often their research and development is flimsy to say the least, but they know only too well that the public are well known for their built-in acceptance if something is positioned with authority and never bothering to check up on this kind of backup data whether it be clinical or scientific claims the companies happen to be making.

Poems / Explanations

FIRST WORLD VS. THIRD WORLD

Aren't you just sick of hearing about war and starvation?
When we've so many problems here in our own nation
Life changing issues affecting each and every one
So now I'm on a mission, I've got my angry head on.
Some countries use up all their own water, they haven't got a clue,
Then they have the cheek to knock on our door, to ask me and you
For a whole two days now, Co-op's had no Typhoo
How am I supposed to survive without my daily brew?
Every kind of bread except the one that I always need,
All your French sticks and wholemeal sprinkled in seeds,
'Scuse me I'm aware people are starving. And that's not right
But I can't have me toast, without my Warburton white!
And that's not all, they keep moving things around
I feel like I'm scrambling through the lost and found
As far as I'm concerned, jam's in aisle ten.
Oh no, not any longer, been bloody moved again,
I've seen on the telly people dodging bombs and guns
But this new layout, I can't find my hot cross buns!
In African nations, they'll queue up for a bowl of rice
They'll not be queueing at Morrisons, seen their fuckin' price?
Don't bang on to me about war and starvation
When I find myself in these untenable situations
People shakin' buckets at me, for another donation
Well, they can go and do one, what with 10% inflation
Got myself a fancy new phone so I can order online
Tapped in all my details thinking all would be fine,
Could only get a dodgy signal between the cereals and the wine
When I got home they'd sent someone else's instead of sending mine!
Such a challenging day, and now I've had it up to here,
I'll be on to customer services and soon put a flea in their ear
Now I'm sat at home with no toast and no brew watching News at Ten
Absolutely nothing about the state of Morrisons...
Just war and starvation all over again.

With so many terrible things happening around the world across many different countries, from war to social and economic devastation caused through political unrest and natural disasters ending with inevitable starvation, destitution, and loss of lives, this poem takes a cynical look at how we compare our own 'misfortunes' in life with the relatively insignificant issues which we are occasionally faced with. How many times do you hear people moaning in the supermarkets because of the absence of certain products they happen to be looking for? It's an easy trap to fall into and I am no exception, but I think sometimes we need to take stock of reality and think oh well things could be a lot worse. We do tend to be a nation of moaners though, it's not unusual to hear people returning from foreign holidays to be heard saying 'the flight was delayed, the hotel was rubbish, and we couldn't eat the food, it was too hot, the sand was too sandy, and the water was too wet, apart from that we had a great time and we've re booked for next year'. 'First World v Third World' really revolves around how we tend to fall into a rant far too prematurely, often without any real justification, and over comparatively minor issues.

HELICOPTER PARENTS

Don't run too fast	it might start that cough
Don't go on that swing	you might fall off
Don't go near the sandpit	there's a two foot drop
Don't go on the ladder	you might get to the top
Don't roll on the grass	it could make you sneeze
Don't crawl through the tunnel	you'll graze your knees
Don't go on those monkey bars	you might get stuck
Stay off that big slide	it's always caked in muck
If you do play footy	be in no later than five
Don't head the ball	you'll have dementia before you're 25
Take those new trainers off	they'll get covered in mud
Put you're old ones on	they'll look just as good
Don't go near the big lake	what do you mean why?
Because I said so	so don't even try
No you're not getting any money	I've got none to spare
Have a lovely day and don't forget	do take care!

Poems / Explanations

Mal Bibby

Modern day parents seem to fall into two completely different categories. There are those who are so engrossed on their phones and into social media that they are almost oblivious to what their children are doing or even where they are. They seem to treat the children as though they were very much an afterthought and almost in the way of their own lives. I have seen some terrible situations where toddlers have been left to wander around, ride scooters or bikes way ahead of their parents along major busy roads, or otherwise act like a petite Rambo while the parent so often appears to be unable to look away from their screens. This I find not only disturbing to watch but socially unacceptable given that there are so many possible dangers, and I will never understand it. Children are such a massive commitment in life and parents should feel fully accountable for their welfare and wellbeing while they are so young and vulnerable. Then on the other end of the spectrum there are the over cautious parents where my poem 'Helicopter Parents' picks up the story. It's short and self-explanatory, and hopefully will bring a smile to those who read it, but hopefully for the right reasons.

20/20 HINDSIGHT

Could've, would've, should've
    if I'd have concentrated and paid a bit more attention
    perhaps spent less time in the teachers detention

Could've, would've, should've...
    if I'd have been a bit more focused and not acted so daft
    been good at maths instead of arts and craft

Could've, would've, should've...
    if I'd have had a higher ambition than to be a bingo caller
    Not been so short and maybe a little taller

Could've, would've, should've...
    if I'd have done more of this instead of too much of that
    Been a little thinner and lost some of that fat

Could've, would've, should've...
    if I'd have looked like someone else and not like me
    had a full head of hair and not follicle free

Could've, would've, should've...
    If only I'd have turned left instead of making a blind right
    if I hadn't have always waited for 20/20 hindsight

Could've, would've, should've if I'd have walked before I learnt to run
But would've, would've, would've it been as half as much fun?

Poems / Explanations

The majority of us are in the generous position of being able to guide our lives by our own decision-making process, however, I do believe that there is also a lot of fate included like 'right place, right time' and certain happenings in our lives lead us to make decisions, safe or otherwise, which may lead us into a change of direction. When I put '20/20' together I was really reflecting on a story my mum told me many years ago about why we lived where we did in our corporation flat and how things could have been very different had my father been a little more adventurous in his decision making. My dad worked in a margarine factory owned by Levers, and many will be aware of Port Sunlight Village which was built by Lord Leverhulme in the 19th century to accommodate and care for his workforce which boasted its own school, church, health centre, community hall and art gallery which created a whole different kind of community based upon this innovative masterpiece. After so many years of employment in the Lever empire houses were offered to employees who qualified and as they became vacant. My mum would have loved to move out of the flat when the opportunity came but my dad stuck with the 'safe' option of our council flat. So, in no way is '20/20' looking back in regret at all but more like 'what if' had alternative decisions been taken which would have meant a different school for me, different friends, and probably different opportunities.

Poems / Explanations

LET'S WRITE ABOUT SOMETHING HAPPY

I want to write something happy so I'd better not watch any news
There's nothing happy on there regardless of anybody's views
I want to write something happy so I'd better not pick up the paper
There's nothing happy in there too long in the tooth for any of that caper
I want to write something happy so I'd better not listen to the radio
There's nothing happy on there just like telly the same old status quo
I want to write something happy I'd better stay away from social media
It's all fake news the poor man's encyclopaedia
I want to write something happy I'm really picking my brain
I look out of my window it's pouring down with rain
I want to write something happy there's the postman at the door
Another brown envelope British Gas want even more
I want to write something happy there's a digital ding on my phone
My rent's overdue again that bastard won't leave me alone
I want to write something happy but I feel I'm in a long queue
I want to write something happy so I'm just going to think about you

Believe it or not, that was my objective when I sat down at the computer to write this short piece, but the more I tried to think of reasons to be happy the less I could find. It's almost like a guilty feeling that with so many bad things happening right now across the world it wouldn't be appropriate to be writing any happy stuff. So, I didn't.

DON'T WORRY

My eyes aren't what they used to be the optician said it's ocular degeneration
He said don't worry it's just an age related complication
Now to read anything I have to make some special preparation
A magnifying glass in one hand and books held at a certain elevation
I've been feeling tired lately doctor said it's probably my circulation
He said don't worry it's just an age related complication
So I've got a hospital appointment for another consultation
Doctor said I'd probably benefit from some kind of vascular operation
I've not been able to walk very far of late doctor said it'll be inflammation
He said don't worry it's just an age related complication
It'll be arthritic pain caused by chronic joint degradation
Doctor said plod on, gave me tablets and said do all in moderation
Going to the toilet is becoming a bit of a problem I've developed constipation
Doctor said don't worry it's just an age related complication
I said I get perineal warmth which is a very strange sensation
He said I need more fibre and gave me some powerful medication
Been a bit hard of hearing since my last big birthday celebration
Doctor said don't worry it's just an age related complication
He took a long look inside and said could I still hear any conversation
I got a bit distressed as I thought he mentioned some kind of amputation
Teeth aren't looking so good so I went to my dentist with some anticipation
She said don't worry it's just an age related complication
NHS doesn't cover the cost of this kind of treatment
                                    so she gave me a quotation
I said are you havin' a laugh, does that cover same day delivery and
                                    full installation
Whenever I get emails or post it's always about prepaid funerals and
                                    cremation
I'm not going to worry as I guess it's just another age related complication

As time goes by it's inevitable that aspects of our health may deteriorate and my body is proving to be no exception to the rule. The last time I had my eyes tested the optician very pensively said 'oh they're not too bad for someone at your stage of life', which is not the most positive or encouraging line to use and almost making it sound like I wouldn't be needing the use of my eyes for much longer, conjuring up images of white sticks and guide dogs in my mind! Similarly when presenting at the doctors with a dodgy knee recently and he said 'well it doesn't look that bad for your age' as though that somehow is going to make me feel better about struggling to walk and I'd say 'oh well that's alright then just get me a wheelchair' and vanish back into the mist. I've actually had the experience where a hospital doctor, after looking at an x-ray of my knee has said to me, 'well I've seen a lot worse', and I have absolutely no doubt that is the case but it comes across as if I'm making it up or looking for some kind of sympathy. 'Don't Worry' is just based upon these kind of situations.

Poems / Explanations

Don't Forget to Vote

Truss, Rishi, Boris or May, if one say's it's night the other will say it's day
They'd lie to their mothers just to get their own way, as we watch
our country fall into decay
The rich get richer and the poor remain poor, yet we still have cutbacks
to 'save' even more
Can anyone tell me what we're saving up for, the only thing I can think of is
war bloody war
Strange we seem to invade countries with oil, ignoring whole continents
fuelled by strife and toil
It's all about power and money we invade their soil, ask the politicians
watch them lie and recoil
More crime than ever, less police on our streets, people staying at home
fearing who'll they meet
Apparently there's no need to worry, we're told it's all good and so there's
no need to retreat
They whip up support from dawn to sundown, to gain control of our
a cities and towns
Looking sincere with their theatrical frowns this bunch of fraudulent
overpaid clowns
It's time to leave now and get your coat, the polls are open and it's that
time to vote
Put your cross against the rudderless boat it's just a lottery like the
Grand National tote

Yes, here I am again on my political soapbox. 'Don't Forget to Vote' is directly linked to my dad. As he got older his motivation to vote waned quite considerably, but I always used to make a point of going round for him, picking him up and taking him to the polling station to place his vote. The very last time this happened before he lost his mobility I went round in my usual manner and gave him the old 'c'mon dad get your coat on it's time to vote'. His response was 'no I can't be bothered' to which I replied in frustration 'well I've been bothered to come round for you and give you a lift'. He looked up at me and said, 'I've been voting and paying my taxes for 60 years or more and the only difference I can honestly see is that I now have an inside toilet'. I thought wow, yes, I could see where he was coming from through his eyes and although we know that standards of living have improved it served to remind me just how long it takes to make change happen. I will keep exercising my right to vote!

Polling
Station

Poems / Explanations

Me, You, Us, Them

No-one can offer a simple explanation
In this unforgiving, bloodthirsty generation
What is the trigger for their motivation
To inflict the ultimate and final devastation
Phone, keys, knife
Why do so many fall into the temptation
With a high price to pay for just one man's elation
In this life we are all trustees
Responsible for causing every social disease
Phone, keys, knife
We only have ourselves to condemn
So it's me, it's you, it's us, it's them
Let's begin to think more of each other
Let's offer hope to each and every mother
Think brother, think sister, think wife
Think phone, think keys, think life

This isn't some kind of clever play on pronouns, but more about accountability. There is absolutely no doubt, whatever statistics are produced, violence, and knife crime in particular, is not only increasing but almost accepted as the 'norm' in our community. Members of the public including schoolchildren being murdered in broad daylight and young people packing knives into their bags alongside their homework, lunch boxes and phones. The powers that be, including politicians, the police and schools all seem to have no clue as to where to begin to take control of this situation. We are all standing by and watching our day-to-day existence crumble into this feral, dog eat dog society. 'Me, You, Us, Them' is really an extension of my poem called 'A Broken Society' and although both sadly reflect where we are at the moment in life, a lot of things have got to change.

Poems / Explanations

MONSTER IN THE CORNER

I've really lost faith in my 48" flat screen,
Force fed programmes which I've already seen.
It used to cost me twelve quid a month to watch TV,
Now it's twelve hundred a year, with a lot less to see.
We all fell hook line and sinker for the switch to Freeview.
What we didn't see hiding was Sky, Sky Plus, and Sky Q,
As the moguls lay in waiting to pillage the poor,
Guiding us like sheep through that big digital door.
Having grown tired of the repeats shown on the BBC,
Millions signed up for this new generational TV,
Now paying extra for the luxury of 'Dave' and 'Gold',
Who stream all day repeats of comedy from old.
If I flick the remote to find a documentary about crime,
'To watch this channel please subscribe to... Amazon Prime'.
Then I stumble across a programme which really interests me,
'To watch this channel please subscribe to... Apple TV'.
So now I'm feeling so cheated I could almost cry.
When I get a digital ding from those nice people at Sky
'Hey congratulations you've been promoted to a Sky VIP!
Switch your broadband to us and get your WIFI free'
That gives me an unsurmountable problem. If I walk away from BT
I won't be able to watch my beloved Blues the next time they play LFC
I've got a twenty-four-month contract from which I cannot break free
As that 48" monster laughs as it stares back at me.
Now I've got both Sky and TNT sport, in ultra HD,
I've got Britbox, Netflix, Apple TV,
Amazon Prime, Virgin, and Disney Plus...
Now I need 'We Buy Any Car.com' because
With the cost of these, I'll be on the bus.

Poems / Explanations

Not so many years ago, television was a luxury beyond the reach of most people. Yet like so much technology, competition brought more affordable products to the marketplace. Now, television isn't the only form of media trying to grab out attention. Innovations such as 'Wi-Fi' and 'smart televisions' have completely changed the landscape to a point where our televisions have become an integral part of our lives. Such a lucrative marketplace inevitably attracts 'the money' and, as the number of available channels and services has now expanded almost out of control, so has the cost. The BBC which has always relied upon the licence fee to produce programmes expanded their network into BBC 1,2,3 and 4 and the commercial channels ITV, Channels 4 and 5 relied upon advertising and sponsorships to fund their output. Then the digital world popped up into our lives which we all bought into having been sold the concept of improved quality, better service, and more choice. 'Monster in The Corner' picks up the story from there.

Poems / Explanations

ALWAYS TAKE A LIST

I was right out of cereal
I needed to replenish
Got myself to Tesco
Cereals stacked high
So, should I go for Puffed Wheat
Go for the malted
Honey nut bakes
Sugar coated flakes
How about low-fat low sugar
Or the healthy muesli
Dried coconut flakes, bananas
Or should i just go commando
I'm beginning to wonder
As I look up and notice
All the Rice Krispies are on offer
But do I go chocolate blueberry
What do I need most here
Fruit and Nut granola
Porridge or Alpen
Honey Nut Cornflakes
Tired of sifting through acres
Ended up with my old favourite
I ventured home in a hurry
Opened the door on the fridge to find

So I go off to the shop
My Snap Crackle and Pop
Soon found the aisle
For a quarter of a mile
Or maybe try the Monster Munch
Or the Double Dipped Crunch
Or the Raspberry Loops
Or the Strawberry Hoops
Cholesterol Busters
With natural nut clusters
And raisins in the mix
With good old Weetabix
Whether I really do care
I'm only halfway there
I suddenly noted
Or yoghurt coated
Vitamin C or vitamin A
Or maybe Special K
And raisin wheats too
What am I going to do ?
Of all the stacks and packs
A large box of sugar smacks
All pleased with myself
No milk on the shelf

Poems / Explanations

This is a direct reflection on a time, after my mother died, when I found myself wanting to support my father more and part of that support was his weekly shopping trip. My mum had always given my dad a list of messages to do when she was alive, which he would diligently go out and quite happily complete, bring home the said items and all was good. When my dad found himself on his own, like many people, he tended to neglect things like shopping until he found himself without. I travelled around the UK for my job which involved staying away, and it was not unusual for me to receive a call from dad at 7.30 at night when I would be eating in a hotel somewhere like Birmingham and he'd say, 'I've got no bread' to which my obvious reply would be 'Well I can't do anything about that now!'

The outcome of these calls was that before each shopping trip, I would ask my dad to make a list of what he required the next time we went out to get his groceries. He never did, and it used to frustrate me, as we'd end up aimlessly wandering around the supermarket and inevitably buying things which he'd forgotten he already had in his fridge and forgetting what he really needed. This poem is a humorous take on that situation but also looks at the ridiculous number of choices we have become familiar with in our supermarkets today, because if you don't take a list of specific items which you require, the potential outcome is, you will either struggle to make a decision or you will end up with multiple impulse purchases (which the supermarkets love of course). It also reminds me of a line in one of George Harrison's songs which he wrote 'If you don't know where you're going, any road will take you there'.

Poems / Explanations

THAT TABLE

I love a cup of coffee and a fresh warm croissant in my local Café Nero
It's a treat I enjoy when my bank balance occasionally climbs above zero
Last time I walked in and looked for a seat, there was only
                    one place left available
Oh no no , please, not that two-seat wobbly wooden table
I should have smelt a rat as soon as I saw the empty space
Why was no-one else sitting there in what appeared to be a perfectly
                    nice place
My nanna was the only thing on earth who was more predictably unstable
I've paid now, I've got no option except to sit at that two-seat
                    wobbly wooden table
I've wedged the wobbly leg with the only serviette I could find in the shop
That didn't work so now I'm clinging tight hold in a bid to make
                    the wobbling stop
Now I can't eat my croissant, but so far all the coffee's still in the cup
But the cup's so full I need two hands to pick the damn thing up
To free up my hands I lifted my knee to meet the underside of the table
In the hope that this balancing act would keep it all relatively stable
Things were going well until the knife decided to slide off my plate
I tried to catch it but I was point seven of a second too late
Dropped my knee right down and knocked the table with my arm
Now my croissant's soaked in coffee while I'm trying to stay cool and calm
Knife's still on the floor, there's more coffee on the table than
                    what's left in the cup
Croissant's not worth eating and no serviette's around to help me mop up
I'm now stranded behind that two-seat wobbly wooden table
When I get up to move out I catch my foot on next doors laptop cable
I've now reached the point, and made the decision, it'll be Café Nero no more
As I look down to see his almond slice and brie pannini staring up at me
                    from the floor

When I look at how powerful the marketing has become behind coffee shops in the UK from 'Starbucks', 'Costa', 'Nero', 'Pret', plus all of the independent coffee shops which have popped up, along with cafes in large stores like Ikea and M&S, I begin to believe how really easy it is to brainwash us all. If I had told my mum that I was going to pay over £3.50 for a cup of coffee and that they were going to force the indignity upon me to queue up for it in a line, her response would have been: 'Go next door!'

But as we all know, there is no next door any longer because our brains have been programmed into 'got to have my freshly made latte'. The profits these companies make are obnoxious and when compared to the mini mum wage and zero-hour contracts they place upon their employees, we're all guilty of supporting their policies. 'That Table' is a look at how they shoehorn as many tables as possible into their outlets. After having to queue up and pay extortionate prices, trying to find a seat can often be a real problem in these coffee emporiums/cattle markets.

Poems / Explanations

No Comprende

Living the costa-del-dream, on a shoestring budget
There'll be no 'stop the planes' over there even though
the Spaniards begrudge it
My friends in blighty are all a bit too quick to judge it.
'Cos we're loving the Spanish lifestyle on our shoestring budget
Our super deluxe accomodation isn't perfect but it didn't break the bank.
It's just unfortunate that we've been pitched next to the camp's sceptic tank,
Our dream on wheels isn't quite like the picture we were shown in the book.
The views we were promised aren't there, whichever way we look.
It's a compact space and although my wife's not as big as her mother,
Wherever we sit or stand, we're always next to each other
But it's our piece of paradise and we've dressed the windows
with little Spanish nets,
So no-one can peep through, in case we're clicking our castanets
A man comes round in a little white van, every single day
We can get real Cadbury's chocolate, and proper 'English' Nescafe.
It all costs us next to nothing, and we really do live well
Fish and chips twice a day, with a gallon of San Miguel.
Beer bellies and tats, 10 hours in the hot blazin' sun,
We've all got faces, like a burnt hot cross bun
Stuff the UK but keep sending that pension to me
And the heating allowance please, it might drop below 40 degrees
We can't speak the lingo but so far we know that 'si' means yes.
We've not bumped into anyone Spanish so we really couldn't care less
Wife's happy she's making a fortune but we daren't tell the tax,
She's got a little parlour for painting nails, or a special Brazillian wax.
She loves posing around in her little convertible Twingo,
Cheap prosecco on tap, botox and bingo
Saturdays market full of tat, before the drag act down the club
Then a jug of traditional Spanish sangria in our favourite English pub
Everywhere we look we can get a meal and a drink for less than a few quid
But we steer clear of that foreign muck like paella, octopus or squid
We adore the Andalucian culture of a traditional Sunday roast or KFC
Premiership football all day, then we go home and watch the BBC.

Mal Bibby

Our 'stay slim, keep trim' classes are a lot more relaxed over here
For five extra euro's, our efforts get rewarded with pizza and beer
Every weeknight there's a top-class tribute act in our social hall.
Monday was Johnny 'What's Another Year' Logan and tonight it's Bobby Ball
Despite the sceptic tank issue and our very limited accommodation,
Our 'Costa-Del-Dream' experience is exceeding our expectations
So now we've no intention at all of ever returning to the UK, that is unless
The time arrives for our hip replacements, then we'll come and milk the NHS.

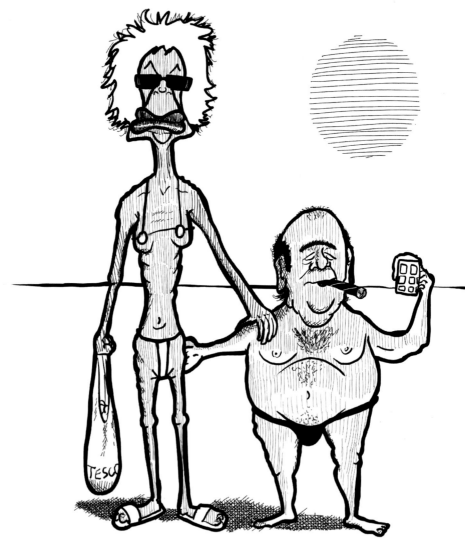

Poems / Explanations

This poem is really about 'mass migration'. Yes, like most people in the UK, I wish the government would get a grip on the current immigration crisis with a more manage able and sensible approach. The thing is: any migrants will always naturally congregate. It seems perfectly normal to me that if I found myself in another country then it would be beneficial to me if I could find another person who either was British or at least could speak English in order to give me some kind of guidance.

Immigration is a hot topic at the moment and so with this poem, I've put the boot on the other foot, as it were, to highlight how Northern France and Southern Spain have become dominated with the British invasion, much to the dislike of the French and Spanish. If I were intending to permanently live in another country, it would be my first priority to learn the language. If for example I was intending to move to Italy, I would not only want to be able to communicate with the locals in their own tongue, but I would want to live, eat, and drink like the Italians do and totally embrace their culture out of respect to them, and for my own knowledge, enjoyment, and overall benefit. The high temperatures throughout the year right across Southern Spain make them the most popular destinations for the Brits to go and live. Camps full of portacabins, tents, and SUVs have developed and have expanded into some of the more popular towns in Spain. Yet 'embracing the culture' seems to be far removed from the objectives of the British expats. In fact, they appear to want to create a 'Little Britain' and I think the poem picks up from there. Enjoy!

Poems / Explanations

LETTER TO NUMBER 10?

Dear Mr. Sunak, I know you're really busy shuffling your stocks and shares
Or organising your favourite weekly game of ministerial musical chairs
However, it is my duty to bring to your attention that this country is in a mess
From our broken social network, our schools and our once revered NHS
The public are supposed to look up to ministers and people of their ilk
It's difficult to build trust when careers only last as long as a bottle of milk
A government bereft of accountability, yet experts at apportioning blame
If you were a thoroughbred racehorse, you would be shot for being lame.
If you were that dead racehorse I doubt you'd make one decent tube of glue
I also ought to remind you Mr. Sunak that none of us actually voted for you
So who is in charge of this mess? Who exactly are pulling the strings?
Just another one of your little devious mechanisms to punish us underlings?
We've got profiteering like never before with increases of 100% and more
Inflation on the rise, yet you expect our doctors,
                                    nurses and teachers to accept less than 5
Bank of England are blaming Westminster, and you blame Ukraine
While the rest of Europe blame Russia for extinguishing the economic flame
So 12 years hasn't been long enough for the Tories to bring some stability
Would that be a lack of trying Mr. Sunak, or a fundamental lack of ability?
We've seen 'dozy Dora May', court jester Boris
                                    and the incompetent 49 day 'less Trust'
What we've witnessed so far Mr. Sunak,
                                    you'll be happy to throw us all under the bus
The old rats have predictably crawled their way back into your sceptic tank
What with Hancock now a tv celeb and laughing his way to the bank
It's hard to deny that Westminster has become nothing more
                                    than a complete and utter farce
So Mr. Sunak please accept this invitation
                                    to shove your Tory polices up your Tory arse.

Poems / Explanations

Directly linked to 'What Have We Got', this poem is a further exposure of the appalling track record this current government has got to show for itself after such a lengthy period in office. From Thatcher to the latest feeble incumbent, successive Conservative governments appear to unashamedly limp from crisis to crisis and somehow still survive the storm.

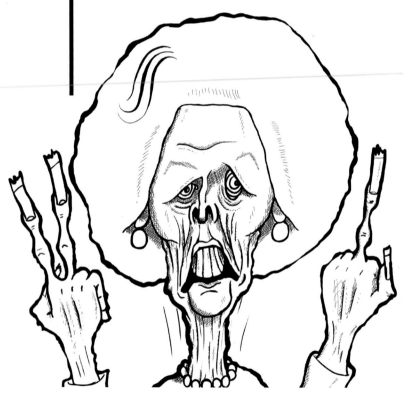

THE FINANCIAL QUAGMIRE

When time has passed all opportunities gone
Your successes and failures blend into one
It's hard to believe that your time is now done
One who has lost and not one who has won
Promises are made in such a confident way
The options are simple and guaranteed to pay
You'll have no regrets he'll reassuringly say
So you tick the box with yes and make his day
30 years fly by and you're told it's all on track
Until the final push exposes some unscheduled slack
Would it have been better under the bed in a sack?
But you ticked the box and now it looks black
As you reflect upon choices made based on pure trust
Followed his recommendation when he 'advised' that you must
Those solid foundations have now crumbled to dust
As your financial alchemist has turned your gold into rust

The standard state pension in the UK is nothing short of a bad joke. We are way behind so many other countries who are often viewed to be below the UK in their financial status but who nonetheless look after their elderly so much better. I have a lot of unanswered questions also about company and private pensions which is anything but a level playing field plus the government and civil service departments where pensions are taxpayer subsidised, all of which offer vastly different outcomes at the end. Staying in a job for life is now virtually impossible for most youngsters today unless qualified as a top professional, but what that means in real terms as people are forced from job to job their company pension pots can become terminally damaged. The average person in the street if asked how pensions work would probably struggle to answer in any depth as indeed, I did. I moved from company to company and always paid pension contributions, but along the way my 'pension pot' got pushed from pillar to post with invisible conditions over which you have little or no control like 'transference fees', 'loss of terminal bonuses' due to moving it to another company, 'loss of fund value' where transferring for example £10k into a different fund for a new employer would only buy £7k worth 'because it's a 'higher quality fund'. How does that work? These pension pots become a haven for the people and companies operating them because they appear to be the only ones who understand how they work, and they know how to work the system. This to any young person won't mean a great deal but it is very important, as the government keep moving the goalposts and retirement ages keep on rising, that there will be more people facing destitution in later life unless a fairer system is introduced, and more companies need to be held to book over how they sell and run these pensions.

Poems / Explanations

Mal Bibby

CHRISTMAS IS ON THE WAY

We've got streamers hangin' down, balloons floating up
Reindeers on the roof, a river of booze to sup,
Tree delivered today, the wreath's on the door
Front room's a grotto, you're still bringing more
Christmas is coming, but all the birds have got flu.
I like vegetables, but I want me slice of turkey too.
Presents all wrapped, emergency booze in the shed
Not a single bird available, because they're all dead.
Pigs in blankets, well they won't go with lamb,
Sage and onion stuffing, well that won't go with ham.
I ain't putting roast beef on the plate, next to cranberry sauce.
If I don't serve a proper Christmas dinner, I'll be wracked with remorse
I've tried Tesco, Sainsbury's, and Iceland frozen foods
Not a turkey in sight because of the avian flu.
I'm on a hotline to Bernard Matthews, but I'm in a queue
Recorded message telling me I'm customer number 4922.
Stop telling me I'm a valued customer. and your staff are so busy
Pull your finger out, and get me that bird in time for Crissy
2 hours and five minutes later, I finally got through
To hear those magic words, 'what can I do for you?'
A flu free turkey please, and let's make it a big one
Sorry sir the last has just been sold, to customer number 4921
Things are now beyond desperate, they're looking downright bleak
I'll now settle for anything with feathers, two wings and a beak
Everyone did get fed at Christmas, without any complaints on the big day
Here-on-in lies my problem, with the legal branch of the RSPCA
It's all to do with next door's cockatiels and his prized African grey
I simply misunderstood when he asked me to 'take care of them'
while he was away.

I am taken by surprise, stupidly, every single year when our shops start their Christmas campaigns just after the summer has gone. I am not a religious person, but I am disappointed in how the commercial aspect of Christmas has reached a point where people refuse to be 'outdone' they simply won't take no for an answer. They will go into extreme debt with credit cards or any means they have in order to be seen to be having a wonderful Christmas and 'giving' their children everything they ask for. Although I have never ventured down the debt route, I have been guilty of being drawn into the commercial pressures with my own children. I have a poem in this book called 'From Dad' which if you read the explanation paints an incredibly different picture to how he was raised back in the day and exactly what Christmas meant to him and his siblings. 'Christmas is on the Way' was penned in 2022 when avian flu was having such an impact on the availability of turkeys when all of a sudden 'panic' affected the marketplace, and so although the poem is fictional it is a combination of people's tenacity to get what they want during difficult times, refusing to be second best, but also hopefully adding a humorous spin on the scenario.

Poems / Explanations

Just Be You

I am as good as you, and you are as good as me
We are not in competition, we are equal, we are free
Refuse to be judged, by what others choose to see
Stand up and be counted, whoever, wherever you may be
Dig deep, be brave, reveal your true identity
Show who you are, and just how strong you can be
Let all the bad fruit drop, for one and all to see
It's the roots under the ground that give the strength to the tree
Take advice from your peers, and guidance from the old
Make your own decisions, don't be controlled
Clarify your thoughts, and you won't get fooled
Justify your actions so you can't be ruled
Ignore that white elephant about going the 'extra mile'
Do things at your pace, in your own unique style
Stand out from the shadows, be honest, be true
Shine like the diamond you are, and just be you

Mal Bibby

I wrote a poem called 'Differences' which was published in my previous book of poems called 'Perspective'. It was largely based upon the positive or negative effect that 'differences', through choice or otherwise, can make between us all and how we perceive those differences and ultimately accept or reject them. 'Just Be You' is an extension of that poem and is targeted towards anyone who may suffer from confidence issues about the way they look or their ability levels within whatever or wherever they are in their lives at any moment in time.

The pressures exerted from marketing advertisements and of course social media platforms is incredible and sometimes underestimated, particularly on the younger generation, about how we should look, what we should be wearing, what we should eat, what happens to be currently 'trending'. The list goes on and on. It causes many people to doubt themselves because they don't feel that they fit into 'the box' or 'any box'. This level of pressure has developed into so much anxiety and varying depressive conditions, contributing to the country's current mental health crisis. 'Just Be You' is a reminder that all of us have something valid to offer in life.

THE WORLD IS OUR STAGE

This life of ours is just a short play
Each acting out scenes from day to day
None of us have written nor read the script
The whole thing's ad lib, from cradle to crypt
Once the curtain is up and the spotlights go on
No matter what happens...the show must go on
Not all of us can produce, not all can direct
The outcome of some scenes are not what you expect
There are no limits on tickets, admission is free
There'll be no choice of standing, or 'vip'
Step into the theatre, don't think you'll spectate
All are included, all participate
You can be ensemble, or choose to take the lead
Each and everyone of us have such a different need
Stand in the footlights, shout and be heard
Or fade in the shadows, if you've come unprepared
An outstanding performance offers no guarantee
A few may understand, but some will never see
So never be fooled, by looks or by age
Life is full of surprises. Up there on that stage
As the final curtain drops and the footlights begin to fade
You'll be defined by the footprint which only you have made.

This is a poem that looks at the world from a theatrical perspective, imagining that we are all born into roles. The more I think about life that way, the more it feels like that is reality. There are very gifted people in every society and the odd 'genius' turns up every now and then in different fields, but, on balance, most of the skills we gain in life are largely from learned behaviour. The majority of us are very fortunate to be able to make our own decisions and the outcome of those decisions helps to plot the direction our lives take, together with the risks and opportunities we choose to follow. 'The World is our Stage' is really a nod towards that reality and we have to make up our own scripts as we go along, produce and direct our own 'performances', and, in the end, be accountable for the outcome of the 'performance' we give.

Poems / Explanations

ACKNOWLEDGEMENTS

A big thank you to Tom Stocks, Carla Mellor and Charlie Staunton who have encouraged and supported me along my spoken word journey, and to my good friend and musical buddy Tony Williams.

I also want to thank the many poets and spoken word artists on the open mic circuit I have had the pleasure to perform alongside at the Shakespeare North Theatre, Prescot; The Williamson Art Gallery, Birkenhead; Clitheroe Castle; Haigh Country Park Wigan; The Spinners Mill Leigh; The Everyman Theatre Liverpool,;The Jacaranda Liverpool; Bolton Open Market; Liverpool Festival of Arts; West Kirby Arts Centre; the Wirral Poetry Festival, and many other venues.

A special thank you to David Waywell for his brilliant illustrations and overall contribution towards getting this publication together.

This book is dedicated, most of all, to my family and friends who have also supported me.